'This is a smart, wise well written essay which answers with much common sense and learning one of the biggest questions of our time.'

Chris Patten, Chancellor of Oxford University and former Governor of Hong Kong

'In this brief but thought-provoking book, acclaimed China specialist Jonathan Fenby challenges and punctures a number of myths about China's rise and offers valuable insights into its current dilemmas and unpredictable future. A stimulating "must read" for all observers of the China scene.'

David Shambaugh, George Washington University and the Brookings Institution

'Jonathan Fenby has managed a highly impressive feat: within a short and elegant text, he has pinpointed the real challenges facing China today if it is truly to become a global actor that will play a serious role in the coming century. The insights give us a road-map for what we might expect from this superpower in the making. A compelling and essential read from a premier China analyst.'

Rana Mitter, author of *China's War with Japan, 1937–1945: The Struggle for Survival*

'China is a bubble in multiple ways – not least in the way its supposed never-ending rise is interpreted and understood in the west. Jonathan Fenby shows courage and insight in pricking the bubble in this important book.'

Will Hutton, Observer columnist and author of *The Writing on the Wall*

'Fenby's thoughtful, balanced analysis of what China has achieved, how it has done so, and the challenges ahead is an excellent corrective to the surfeit of overly laudatory and excessively dire assessments of China's future and its implications for the world.'

Thomas Fingar, Stanford University

'In this spirited and insightful book, Jonathan Fenby takes on the China bulls by taking a clear-eyed look at China's dysfunctional political system, which does not appear up to the task of tackling the social, legal, economic, environmental, demographic and security challenges facing the country. Highly recommended.'

Joseph Fewsmith, Boston University, author of *The Logic and Limits of Political Reform in China*

'Leading China commentator Jonathan Fenby's latest book on China's position in the world offers a nuanced picture of the country's strengths and weaknesses.'

China Daily

'Fenby understands to its deepest roots the nature of Chinese Communist Party rule and its effect throughout society. The Party will, therefore, hate his eloquent and merciless dissection of its entire record and performance. But readers new to China should start right here.'

Jonathan Mirsky, *Times Higher Education*

'The development of any country is accompanied by twists and turns. This book is a reminder that it is still too early to position the world at the dawn of a Chinese century.'

Global Times

'Fenby's concise, yet comprehensive, essay should be the first thing read by anyone with an interest - business, political, or intellectual - in the future of China.'

Charles Horner, Senior Fellow, Hudson Institute

'An excellent summary of the broad spectrum of very serious issues China faces in the immediate future.'

Fraser Howie, author of Red Capitalism: *The Fragile Financial Foundation of China's Extraordinary Rise*

Will China Dominate the 21st Century?

Global Futures Series

.

Jonathan Fenby

———

WILL CHINA DOMINATE THE 21st CENTURY?

polity

The right of Jonathan Fenby to be identified as Author of this Work
has been asserted in accordance with the UK Copyright, Designs and
Patents Act 1988.

First published in 2014 by Polity Press

Polity Press
65 Bridge Street
Cambridge CB2 1UR, UK

Polity Press
350 Main Street
Malden, MA 02148, USA

ISBN-13: 978-0-7456-7926-6
ISBN-13: 978-0-7456-7927-3 (pb)

A catalogue record for this book is available from the British Library.

Typeset in 11 on 15 pt Sabon by
Servis Filmsetting Ltd, Stockport, Cheshire
Printed and bound in the United States by Edwards Brothers Malloy

The publisher has used its best endeavours to ensure that the URLs for
external websites referred to in this book are correct and active at the
time of going to press. However, the publisher has no responsibility
for the websites and can make no guarantee that a site will remain live
or that the content is or will remain appropriate.

Every effort has been made to trace all copyright holders, but if any
have been inadvertently overlooked the publisher will be pleased to
include any necessary credits in any subsequent reprint or edition.

For further information on Polity, visit our website:
www.politybooks.com

Contents

1

China's Watershed

China breeds powerful mythologies to impress its own people and awe foreigners. This was the case during the Empire of more than two thousand years when its rulers claimed to be semi-divine holders of the Mandate of Heaven and the Middle Kingdom stood aloof from the barbarians. China's size and relative isolation made it a place of mystery and admiration. If there were major setbacks from the time of the first Opium War of 1839–42, this was held to be all the fault of foreigners in the official narrative of the 'century of humiliation', while China's civilizational values remained superior, its unity within fixed frontiers epitomized by the Confucian cultural homogeneity of the Han race and the imperial civil service with its subtle statecraft. Like most myths, these themes contain elements of truth but are also full of holes.

1

To start with, the idea of Chinese unity within roughly its present borders is controverted by the country's repeated periods of divisions, one lasting for three centuries. Equally, the thesis that the Han have always governed China and ensured its greatness is contradicted by the rule of the Yuan (Mongol) and the Qing (Manchu) dynasties, which held the throne for a combined 375 years of the last 639 years of the Empire. Earlier, the nomadic Jin held sway over northern China for 120 years after exacting tribute from the Song dynasty. The back-up idea that such foreigners became Sinicized is debatable: the Yuan rejected Chinese ways, while the more subtle Qing adopted them to facilitate their control. Both governed multi-ethnic realms of which China was only a part and in which Mongol and then Manchu interests had priority.

Confucianism is held to have been China's lodestar, its philosophical and ethical teachings providing a benevolent route to wisdom and good behaviour for rulers and ruled alike. It certainly has had a major influence, but its benevolence is tempered by the usefulness for those in power of its principle of filial piety, enabling them to claim deference as the fathers of the people to whom obedience is due. Often ignored is the parallel and rival doctrine of legalism, which uses the law to cow citizens into submission, and extols secrecy and charismatic authority. From the First Emperor, who was reputed to have buried Confucian scholars alive, to Mao Zedong's violent anti-Confucianism and today's repression of dissent, legalism never goes away.

The imperial civil service chosen by rigorous examination is presented as having produced an unrivalled administrative meritocracy. But it never mastered the cycle of dynastic rise and fall, often accelerating at a violent pace when a ruling house floundered, as with the Ming in the 17th century. Meanwhile the length and complexity of the supposedly meritocratic civil service examination system meant that successful candidates came mainly from rich and scholarly families – moreover, in the late imperial period, degrees could be bought or were given in return for service. Nor did meritocracy extend to the rulers: emperors took the throne by inheritance or violence. The opposition which admirers of the Chinese system erect today between meritocracy and democracy to argue that the first is more effective than the second is, in any case, a false one – meritocratic progress is a mark of true democracy; it just happens to differ from the Chinese system by allowing people to vote for their rulers.

The 'century of humiliation' between 1839 and

1949 as foreign imperialism 'carved the melon' of China has to be set in the context of far greater suffering from home-grown tribulations: huge mid-19th-century revolts that took tens of millions of lives; hidebound rule by the later Qing; the dynasty's massive mistake in allying with the Boxer movement in 1900; and then the end of the Empire followed by warlord anarchy, weak government and civil war.

Admirers such as Henry Kissinger regard Chinese diplomacy as the acme of subtle, encircling strategy in contrast to the frontal approach of the West. But the statecraft exercised by the Middle Kingdom and its successors brought little success, however elegant in theory.[1] There is also a myth that China was not an expansionist power and was content to exist within its settled borders. So what of imperial campaigns against the Uyghurs, Kazakhs, Kyrgyzs, Evenks and Mongols and invasions of Vietnam, Korea and Burma? Finally, we are told that China is 're-emerging' to regain past global influence.[2] This is to mis-read history. Though imperial China was by no means isolated, it did not play a global role in the way of European empires. Only now is it finding its international path.

But the story of China's past gains powerful backing from the country's extraordinary material rise in the past three decades as the gross domestic product (GDP) went from 364 billion yuan at the start of economic reform in 1978 to 1.5 trillion 10 years later, reaching 10 trillion at the turn of the century and then sky-rocketing past 20 trillion in the middle of the decade to reach 52 trillion (US$8.5 trillion) in 2012. Annual real growth was above 8 per cent in all but eight of the past 35 years. According to the International Monetary Fund (IMF), the People's Republic of China (PRC) accounted for half global growth between 2007 and 2012.

The scale and speed of China's emergence as a major global actor whose economy is set to overtake that of the United States by the end of the present decade has been the most important international event since the end of the Cold War. This has coincided with a time when the West, and in particular the United States, has entered increasingly choppy waters and the post-1945 global balance has eroded. Mao Zedong changed China after the Communist victory of 1949 as the Party filled the vacuum left by the weakness of its Nationalist predecessors and the debilitating economic, social and political effects of the drawn-out conflict with the Japanese invaders stretching back to 1931. But the economic reforms launched by Deng Xiaoping in the late 1970s have reached far wider, radically altering the world with a global impact that the Empire never sought.

Yet China's ascent has bred another set of myths, misapprehensions and easy conclusions that obscure the reality of a country where the basic building blocks of interpretation are often hard to grasp and are wrapped in theory of disputable value – after all, Li Keqiang, the man who became Prime Minister in 2013 said earlier that Chinese economic statistics are 'man made' and, apart from numbers for electricity use, bank lending and rail freight, are 'for reference only'.[3]

Deng, the ultimate survivor who had taken part in the iconic Long March, been political commissar of a major army, implemented Mao's early purges and then weathered his own humiliation during the Cultural Revolution, grasped the need for economic reform and its political purpose after winning the power struggle that followed the Great Helmsman's death in 1976. Delegations sent abroad returned home with word of just how far China had fallen behind as Mao's policies levelled the population down, leading the new paramount leader to remark that 'the more we see, the more we realize how backward we are'.[4]

His motivation was not simply a matter of economics and improved livelihoods. There was an underlying national and political goal. Deng, a patriot who joined the Communist Party in 1923, had been a prominent actor and faithful follower of Mao in the winning of the civil war against the Nationalists, the restoration of national unity, the creation of a governing system and the new economic state-directed course followed after 1949. Though it brought some benefits, for instance in the extension of primitive health care and greater longevity, the growth of the People's Republic was pursued at enormous human cost and with great inefficiencies bred by the reckless pursuit of impossible goals by ill-considered means at the behest of an all-powerful leader who played with the nation as if with a toy.[5]

When he succeeded Mao, therefore, Deng knew that the previous three decades had left an awful legacy as the Great Helmsman sought to impose personal rule in the mould of the First Emperor. The 'storming of the fortress' in the Cultural Revolution consigned the PRC to also-ran status globally and menaced the Party, whose hierarchy had been laid waste by its leader in his wilful exercise of personal power. Poverty was institutionalized. The state was virtually bankrupt. Productivity had slumped. From these depths, the diminutive, chain-smoking Deng set out to make China great again and to ensure that the political movement he served was the unique vehicle by which this could be achieved, drawing

legitimacy from growth and revived national pride while maintaining a monopolistic grip on power.

The story of what followed has been evident since the mid-1990s, though an alternative chorus of doomsayers has forecast the coming collapse of China for more than a decade. Xi Jinping, the leader of China who took over as Party General Secretary, State President and Chair of the Military Commission in 2012–13, now proclaims the pursuit of the 'China Dream', which he defines as being to 'make persistent efforts, press ahead with indomitable will, continue to push forward the great cause of socialism with Chinese characteristics, and strive to achieve the Chinese dream of great rejuvenation of the Chinese nation'.

What does this actually mean? 'To realize the Chinese road, we must spread the Chinese spirit, which combines the spirit of the nation with patriotism as the core and the spirit of the time with reform and innovation as the core,' Xi responds. In California for a US–PRC summit in 2013, he added an international gloss: 'The Chinese dream is about peace, development, cooperation and win-win results, and it is connected to the American dream and beautiful dreams of people in other countries.' The People's Liberation Army (PLA) newspaper was moved to hail the leader's vision as 'like seeing a ship's mast in the sea, like seeing the radiant sun rise in the east . . . the cosmic truth'.[6]

The numbers appear to make forecasts of Chinese domination of the coming decades incontrovertible. Drawing on 800 million workers and $20 trillion worth of material assets, the PRC has become the biggest manufacturer and exporter on earth and the key source of demand for raw materials from around the globe. It accounts for two-thirds of commerce among the major developing economies in the BRIC (Brazil, Russia, India, China)[7] grouping and is the European Union's largest commercial partner. Its trade with Africa has increased tenfold since 2000. Chinese companies are buying into utilities in Britain and Portugal, the Club Med holiday firm and the port of the Piraeus in Greece; they have acquired the Volvo car company and the British Weetabix breakfast cereal firm, and they bid in 2013 for the biggest US pork producer, Smithfield Foods.

Russia reached a $270 billion deal in 2013 to supply the Chinese mainland with oil from Siberia. Rich Chinese snap up luxury property in developed nations and the country's tourists crowd luxury shops in Paris, Florence and London. Its engineering enterprises develop infrastructure around the globe, earning $117 billion in contract revenue in 2012.[8] A Chinese firm is planning to build a waterway across Nicaragua to compete with the Panama Canal, and others have stakes in ports from California to Singapore.[9]

With a population of 1.3 billion, China has more big cities than any other country, the longest high-speed train network, the highest number of tourists going abroad (83 million spending more than $100 billion in 2012),[10] an army of more than 200 million migrant workers and a healthy central government budget balance. Its ruling party has more than 80 million members – if they formed a country of their own, it would be the 16th most populous on the planet – and its Youth League counts 90 million adherents, with 3.5 million grassroots branch organizations.

The PRC is a nuclear power with a permanent seat and veto on the United Nations Security Council. The PLA is the largest standing force on earth with 1.4 million troops – plus a million or more armed paramilitaries. The military budget has grown steadily, rising by 11 per cent in 2012. After centuries as a 'homeland' power which focused on its land territory, the PRC is developing its navy to give it blue water outreach and, it hopes, the capacity to deny the US fleet access to the eastern Pacific. It is building a 'string of pearls' of ports and military outposts stretching along the sea routes on which its energy supplies head from the Middle East. It is fashioning a 'Marching West' policy to strengthen its presence in Central Asia, and considering moving into Afghanistan for that country's mineral reserves when the United States and its allies leave.[11]

Beijing claims the right to reunify with the democratic island of Taiwan by force if need be to recreate the imperial domain of the Qing, pointing more than 1,000 missiles across the Strait between them. It refuses to relax its grip on the non-Han territories of Tibet and Xinjiang, which make up 4.1 million square kilometres out of China's total of 9.6 million but contain only 25 million of the PRC's 1.3 billion inhabitants. No debate is permitted about whether these traditionally non-Han lands occupied by the PLA in the early stages of Communist rule belong to China. Both have been the target of large-scale Han immigration and the destruction of the indigenous culture in the name of modernization. The Dalai Lama and Buddhist monks who staged more than 100 self-immolations between 2009 and 2013 are condemned as 'splittists'. Muslims seeking autonomy in the lands where China meets Central Asia are depicted as terrorists linked to Al-Qaeda.

Mainland China has something to please both left and right. It has pulled more people out of poverty in a shorter space of time than any country in human history and insists on the correctness of Marxism-Leninism-Maoism. But it has little in the way of either welfare provisions or effective regulation, gives business great leeway and cleaves to Victorian values to get people to work hard. Health insurance has been extended to 90 per cent of the population but provides scanty financial coverage, while factory signs warn workers, 'If you don't work hard today, you will search for a job tomorrow.'

China's civilization stretches back for millennia and its largely ethnically unified people (the 55 officially recognized minority groups make up only 8.5 per cent of the population) have inherited a sense of their special place in the world. Even if there are remarkably few buildings from the past (in part because so much was in wood which was burned down in fires or wars), the vestiges of history run through today's national system as the leadership claims a Mandate of Heaven not dissimilar from that of the emperors, even if it is based on economic success and 'scientific socialism' rather than divine favour, and is held by the institution of the Communist Party rather than by a single man.

All of which seems to lead inevitably to the conclusion argued by the historian Niall Ferguson and many others that 'the 21st century will belong to China',[12] a thesis summed up in the title of the book by the British author Martin Jacques: *When China Rules the World*. According to the Pew Institute's Global Attitudes Survey in 2013, the proportion of people ranking the mainland as the world's leading economic power has risen from 20 to 34 per cent since 2008, while those naming the United States as number one has fallen from 47 to 41 per cent. In 23 of the 39 nations covered, majorities or pluralities said China has replaced or will replace the United States in first place; in Britain, 53 per cent and in Germany 58 per cent put the PRC first. Two-thirds of Chinese agreed.[13] Sceptics may recall forecasts in the 1970s of 'Japan as Number One' as its companies roared ahead across the globe and Mitsubishi bought the Rockefeller Center and Sony snapped up Columbia Studios, only for the country then to plunge into its 'lost decade' and more, owing to the imbalances in the economy, high debt levels, a strong currency and domestic stagnation. But proponents of China's dominance maintain that its history and size place it above the troubles that beset its neighbour across the sea.

This book will argue, however, that, far from being an unalloyed source of civilizational strength, these historical inheritances and their current manifestations contain serious weaknesses in a country which, for all the change it has undergone, has reverted again and again to a model that has become outdated, imposing it by force if necessary and unable to contain reasoned debate about progress. This stretches from the confines of the top-down political system, with its equation of dissent with treason, to endemic corruption and the intrusion of the Party State into every area of life, all the way to family planning agents who check on women's menstrual cycles.

Advocates of the China model see it as possessing inherent strengths and prefer to ignore the way that, in the mould of their imperial predecessors, the rulers make a point of maintaining a large repressive apparatus on behalf of the Party State; the budget for internal security is larger than that of the armed forces. Political conformity has been enforced. The protest in Beijing which ended in the army massacre of students and ordinary citizens in June 1989 is officially classed as counter-revolutionary turmoil; to this day, it cannot be discussed openly. When faced with what they regard as a political challenge, the rulers, as usual in Chinese history, fall back on violence, or the threat of it. The argument, accepted by some Western admirers, is that China is simply too big and too complex to be run any other way.

That is quite a stretch, and says something not very flattering about the nature of the country's much-vaunted civilization. The danger to the regime is that, as was repeatedly the case in the imperial past, this mindset becomes a recipe for immobilism which is in increasing conflict with the country's evolution as a whole.

We need to give serious re-consideration to the portrait of China as a country run by a uniquely qualified meritocracy which excels in long-term planning in a regime melding inherited strengths denied to the West with an unprecedented and unstoppable economic trajectory. In another echo of the past, the elite politics of today's China bears a distinct resemblance to the closed courts of the imperial era, which ended with dynastic decline as the cycle of power came full circle – a tradition that took shape from the beginning under the First Emperor, whose reign lasted for only 11 years and was followed by the bloody collapse of the dynasty three years later.

That story is not going to play out any time soon, despite in-fighting behind the screen in the run-up to the 2012 Party Congress which saw the dramatic fall of the maverick politician Bo Xilai. Xi Jinping's accession to the top jobs was duly confirmed and he immediately set out to impose a more forceful leadership style than his predecessor, Hu Jintao, with his 'China Dream' on the back of a crusade against corruption and in favour of frugality of cadres to bring them closer to the people. Those who have been predicting the coming collapse of China for years have been repeatedly discomfited by the country's ability to buck many of the rules of orthodox economics and politics, though short-sellers can still make money out of recurrent outbreaks of bearishness about economic prospects as growth slows.

The Party State has eliminated potential centres of opposition, not only politically, but also in society at large. Lu Xiaobo, the 2010 Nobel Peace Prize winner, was sent to jail for 11 years for organizing a petition in favour of democracy. All conventional media are controlled by the regime, and the censorship office keeps close tabs on the Internet. The middle class has been co-opted into the system by the material comforts it enjoys in the shape of being able to afford urban living, private health care and education plus foreign travel. Blue-collar workers have been given large pay rises and migrants are joining the consumer society.

For all that, six decades after Mao proclaimed the PRC from the balcony outside the Forbidden City and three decades after Deng engineered the change of economic course, China faces a daunting array of challenges. The leadership of Xi Jinping and Prime Minister Li Keqiang recognizes the weakness and the need for action. But they are confronted with a second, equally serious, problem. The changes the PRC needs come with huge difficulties in implementation, while keeping the show on the road is proving to be an increasingly tricky task as the leadership has to manage a slowing economy and avoid the 'middle-income' trap that can block development after the initial growth spurt – though the threat may be a reduced expansion rate rather than paralysis or decline.

The scale of the reform required is enormous, stretching across agriculture, labour, finance, the law, state industries, water and energy pricing – without mentioning political change. The inbred nature of the system put in place since 1949 and given new life by Deng means that changing one element risks knock-on effects that ripple through the power apparatus in a Leninist system in which the Party General Secretary is Chairman and Chief Executive and the Prime Minister merely the Chief Operating Officer of PRC Inc. The top Party board, the Politburo, and its even more elevated Standing Committee out-rank the state government, with its Leading Groups on policy matters enjoying more clout than ministries, its provincial branches superior to the regional administrations, its Disciplinary Commission operating independently of the law. Its ideologues claim wisdom worthy of emperors as Xi Jinping calls on the Party to exhibit the strength of 'metal turned into iron' and to constitute 'the firm leadership core for advancing the cause of socialism with Chinese characteristics'.

Though, as we will see, there are many ways in which the regime falls short of its proclaimed objectives in practice, this single-mindedness makes relaxing the control at the heart of the PRC a hazardous undertaking, with the example of Mikhail Gorbachev and the collapse of the USSR a constant spectre. The politico-economic equation which was Deng's great insight to save the Party is reaching the end of its natural life. But replacing it is made extremely difficult by its internal mechanisms and centralism, which stand in the way of change and give resonance to the prospect of what has been termed a 'trapped transition'.[14] As the World Bank put it in 2012 in a report with which the Beijing government collaborated, 'Significant policy adjustments are required in order for China's growth to be sustainable. Experience shows that transitioning from middle-income to high-income status can be more difficult than moving up from low to middle income'.[15]

Yet the ultimate outcome of the further far-reaching reforms the PRC needs to maintain its momentum could seriously undermine the regime – first in the economy and then with wider social and political repercussions. That is not a prospect which Xi Jinping and his colleagues in the Politburo will easily implement; the new leader's diagnosis of the reasons for the fall of the Soviet Union include his judgement that nobody was left who was strong enough to save the system, the implication being that, in him, the PRC has a doughty defender.

There are significant flaws in the apparently all-conquering combination of the Party State and a civilization stretching back for thousands of years. The former confronts substantial weaknesses while the latter is undermined by a psychological gap in a society which is emboldened by economic progress but unnerved by the nature of that progress, giving rise, for instance, to increasing recourse to religion and practices once condemned as superstition, and creating a 'trust gap' which will recur throughout this book. At the time of the 2012 Party Congress, the leadership's reading list included Alexis de Tocqueville's analysis of the fall of the Bourbon monarchy in France at the end of the 18th century, with its observation that an autocracy is most vulnerable when it starts to reform and that regime change is most likely when improved living conditions give people time to think. 'As a government continues to incite the desire for wealth accumulation, which breeds corruption and saps its moral credibility, prosperity actually plants the seed of the regime's demise,' a commentator in the magazine *Caixin* wrote. 'Economic growth, instead of keeping people content, makes them restive. Thus the 8 per cent rate of GDP growth, long perceived in China as sine qua non for stability, may have the opposite effect. ... Economic progress has lost its magic; equality and justice now matter more. Even the moderates think change must happen to pull China out of stagnation.'[16]

The myths that have accreted as a result of the combination of China's spectacular growth and the advantages perceived to have been inherited from its past obscure a set of challenges every bit as testing as those confronting the West. The economy, which has powered China's rise and aroused such admiration, needs a major re-think, but this comes with big risks, as we will see in Chapter 3. While China has some of the biggest companies on earth, important sectors are fragmented, hindering economies of scale – the top 10 supermarkets, for example, have an 8 per cent market share compared to 75 per cent in the United States, and the largest property firm accounts for 4 per cent of its sector. Provincial governments encourage local champions and prevent consolidation that would reduce wasteful excess capacity. Even the booming export data have been brought into question with the disclosure of tax dodges which inflate the figures and mean that the PRC did not, as was trumpeted, overtake the United States in 2012 to become the biggest trading economy.[17]

There is a major crisis of the environment and degradation of natural resources which is estimated by the World Bank to cost the equivalent of 9 per cent of GDP. Serious air pollution not only affects the health of Chinese citizens but also substantially increases global carbon-dioxide emissions. If the PRC continues emissions at the present rate, it would account for two-thirds of the worldwide total needed to restrain global warming.[18] Meanwhile, the ageing of the population brings the loss of the 'demographic dividend' of young workers coming into the labour force. The trust deficit is augmented by poor safety standards, especially for food, corruption, a weak legal system and yawning personal and regional wealth disparities. Discontent at Chinese rule flares up regularly in Tibet and

Xinjiang. Relations with the United States, Japan and India are scratchy. Other powers are concerned at the sharp increase in the PRC's military budget and nationalism at a time when Beijing is involved in confrontations with other East Asian states. Apart from the defence of certain 'core interests', Beijing generally conducts its foreign policy on a case-by-case bilateral basis rather than assuming the role of a 'global stakeholder' commensurate with its economic clout, keeping an obstinately low profile and leaving it to others to make the running on major issues such as Syria in 2013.

Xi and his colleagues want to create a more prosperous nation with a more sustainable economy enjoying stability under one-party rule. But the enormous material improvement of the past three decades has bred a society that is less ready to follow top-down dictates, with popular protests estimated to number between 150,000 and 180,000 a year and social media playing a key role – the censors may keep watch but the ability to communicate with one another on a massive scale is a game changer in a country where the leadership always seeks to control public discourse. Ensuring stability on its own terms is a key aim of the Party State but its concern about achieving that end is reflected in the increase in the annual domestic security budget by more than 200 billion yuan to 769 billion yuan ($125 billion) since 2010.

These challenges may be surmounted, at least in part. But totalitarian regimes are prone to breed and perpetuate flawed policies, especially when the leaders see them as buttressing the system on which they depend. China is no exception. Even if 'totalitarianism light' impinges less and less on the everyday lives of its citizens, they still have no direct say in decision-making that impacts on their lives. But they live with its consequences.

This breeds an in-built conflict that can only become sharper. It is evident in the economy, as we will see in Chapter 3, and runs through society, as shown in Chapter 4. A watershed is being reached. The leadership may seek to skirt round it in the interests of short-term self-preservation and try to go on as before – as it did for much of the first decade of this century. But the difficulties can only multiply as contradictions pile up, in large part as a result of what has been accomplished, which cannot be easily abandoned without removing the struts that underpin the whole edifice. Change would make China less of an exception, more of a normal nation subject to the stresses normal nations experience, the high-octane, pressure-cooker decades giving way to something more mundane.

China will be one of two major global national players in the years ahead. Its influence will be great both as a consumer and as a producer. But the internal conflicts between society and the regime can only increase while its economy still needs a lot of work. This will be a highly tricky process, demanding maximum attention and skilful handling by Xi and his successors plus adaptation by a regime whose nature makes it hard for it to question its basic tenets as it must if it is to progress.

While China's model was eminently successful at home, it was the product of a unique combination of a huge, cheap flood of workers coming into the labour force; abundant low-cost capital from savings; strong foreign demand for deflationary PRC exports pushed by mercantilist policies; and the liberation of a population yearning for a better life from the constraints of the Maoist years and the suffering and backwardness of the previous century. None of those factors apply today as they did in the last part of the 20th century. Though China has made considerable technological strides, for instance building the world's most powerful computer, it tends to shine in terms of quantity rather than quality: investing heavily in shipyards building big container vessels which nobody wants rather than the higher added-value boats made by Japan and South Korea. Notably, too, a study in 2013 found that 92 per cent of Chinese with American Ph.D.s were still in the United States five years after graduation.[19]

The PRC's record in cutting-edge innovation is poor. In a technology-driven world, that matters a lot. The PRC may have four of the ten largest makers of smartphones but they use technology invented elsewhere. The high-speed train network is based on European and Japanese models. China's automobile industry and much other advanced manufacturing depend on imported expertise. The launch of the PRC's long-planned first big airliner had to be put back for two to three years in 2013. Vital parts, including the engines, have to be bought from abroad and the manager of the project admits to a weakness of technical skills. When it finally flies, the plane will be the equivalent of Airbus or Boeing models introduced two decades earlier – this in a country estimated to need more than 5,000 new commercial aircraft in the next twenty years.[20]

However much authoritarian rulers elsewhere may dream of emulating it, the so-called 'Beijing Consensus' is one of a kind; the conditions of China in the 1980s are not replicable and the world has changed with the contraction of global demand. China's efforts to spread its 'soft power' have been quantitative rather than qualitative; despite the mega-screen showing Chinese television in Times Square, the big spending on English-language media outlets and travelling exhibitions of the Terracotta Warriors and other treasures, there have been few converts to the Chinese way of government.

The PRC's in-built strengths and size will prevent collapse. But this book will argue that the system which has produced such success has within it the seeds, if not of its destruction, then of its own slowing down – and that the political apparatus is ill-fitted to cope with the prospect. There is the danger of a nationalist response to a sharper than expected deceleration in an already volatile region of the world that takes on added importance as the main driver of global growth. But, aside from the threat of that kind, China confronts enormous tests as the economy seeks to rebalance and the leadership faces growing contradictions in the interests of regime preservation and the status quo. As a result, the PRC will not have the economic, political and human resources to dominate the world, even if it wished to do so, and to extrapolate from the ancient and recent past is a facile but flawed game which takes too little account of countervailing factors.

China's concerns are and will be overwhelmingly domestic, above all to manage a decline in the rate of growth to achieve a more sustainable economy. Though these concerns have international aspects, notably in the supply of raw materials, they are essentially inward-looking. Nor is the world of the present the kind of place where one nation can hold sway, as demonstrated by the Cold War division of the globe and the travails of the United States since the Vietnam War. This century will not end in the triumph of the People's Republic any more than the last one did with the enduring victory of the United States.[21]

2

The Political Trap

The reasons why the PRC will not dominate the 21st century involve the economy, politics, social developments and foreign relations. These are all inter-connected because, as explained in the previous chapter, economic growth is a fundamentally political priority and the country's social evolution and its relationships with the rest of the world spring from that political–economic nexus. These themes will be dealt with in this and the next three chapters; it is best to start with the politics since this is at the core of the system that encompasses the other three elements.

The PRC is the last major state on earth run by a Communist Party – and one of only five countries professing adherence to Marxism Leninism or, in the case of North Korea, pursuing its own self-reliance creed. The heads of Marx and Engels look out over Party meetings. Mao's image dominates Tiananmen Square and stares out from virtually all banknotes (as well as dangling on medallions over the dashboard of a fair number of taxis). This may seem anachronistic in a land of rampant consumerism, where the economy uses market mechanisms and displays yawning wealth gaps. The paradoxes crop up all the time.

How can China be a Communist state when Prime Minister Li Keqiang declares that 'we will make an all-around effort to deepen market-oriented reform' and when private enterprise played such a key role in driving growth in the years after Deng's initial reforms? How can China's leaders pay obeisance to the notion of Communist equality when in 2012 the country counted 122 known dollar billionaires, 83 of whom sat in the annual plenary sessions of the national legislature (in all, 500 of the nearly 3,000 legislators came from the business world), and when their own relatives have made fortunes in business through family connections?

Time, one might consider, to re-think the regime's political ideology and its application as the PRC moves into the fifth generation of Communist rule and to pose some pertinent questions. What is the Party for nowadays, and where does its legitimacy lie? Has it become simply a delivery vehicle for material progress? Or is it, rather, a self-preservation machine, claiming the modern Mandate of Heaven with no greater purpose than to hold on to power?

With his public relations savvy and apparent recognition of everyday realities, Xi Jinping would seem well placed to elaborate some answers that will steer China in the years ahead. His life has shown him the vicissitudes of Communist rule. Having been brought up in privileged surroundings as the son of a first-generation Party leader, he was sent down to live in a cave and tend pigs when his father, Xi Zhongxun, was purged during the Cultural Revolution. He was refused Party membership ten times. He recalls this as an emotional time and the Cultural Revolution as an illusion. 'I ate a lot more bitterness than most people,' he reflects.

But, like other children of historic leaders cast out by Mao and rehabilitated by Deng, he became wedded to the regime, studying Marxism-Maoism after being allowed to return to Beijing and becoming 'redder than red', as one friend put it. His subsequent advance through provincial posts to the Standing Committee of the Politburo in 2007 and then to the top three jobs five years later was a smoothly handled ascent aided by multiple contacts in politics, the economy and the military established over the years. He appears more open and self-confident than his predecessor, photographed on a visit to a Yangtze river port in 2013 holding his own umbrella and with his trousers rolled up amid heavy rain.[1] He vaunts his pragmatism, which, he says, took root during the Cultural Revolution 'and still exerts a constant influence on me'. But, to judge by his statements after rising to the very top, he sees ideology as an essential prop for the regime and uses Mao-style language to urge officials to toe the line, as in his injunction in the summer of 2013 to them to 'look in the mirror, groom yourself, take a bath and seek remedies'.[2] ('Look in the mirror' means using the Party constitution as a mirror to help conform to discipline and public expectations; 'groom oneself' means correcting misconduct and projecting a good image; 'taking a bath' means having a clean mind and behaving well; 'seeking remedies' means educating or punishing those guilty of misconduct.)

Xi attributes the collapse of the Soviet Union to a loss of belief in Communism. 'The negation of Lenin and Stalin ... spawned historical nihilism and the confusion of thoughts' with no strong man left to defend the system, he says. Cleaving to Marxism is vital, he adds. Mao Zedong Thought is the foundation of the regime and it is a grave mistake, he argues, to draw a distinction between the Great Helmsman's era and the subsequent time of reform and opening up. Rather, the PRC's history must be seen as a continuum in which the Party never made mistakes. However wrong, the script has its inner logic as it seeks to serve his basic aim of strengthening the Party.[3]

China is in many ways a far freer place for its citizens than at any time since 1949. Material progress and modernity have brought considerable individual liberation. But the security apparatus remains very powerful and has been steadily strengthened in recent years. Police often exercise arbitrary authority and judges are required to swear an oath of loyalty to the Party. Legal liberalization has stopped and the leaders have made it clear that the role of the law is to strengthen the Party – when a new President of the Supreme People's Court took office in 2013, he praised his predecessor for having maintained 'a firm political stand'. Human rights defenders who seek simply to apply the law are 'disappeared', interrogated – sometimes with torture – and can be jailed on the most flimsy of charges. The Nobel Peace Prize winner of 2010, Liu Xiaobo, is, as we noted earlier, in prison for 11 years for having circulated a petition calling for democracy, and his brother-in-law was sent to jail for 11 years, too, for fraud in 2013, a case widely seen as an example of official retribution against the dissident's family.

People who travel from the provinces to present petitions in Beijing may be held in clandestine 'black jails' or incarcerated in psychiatric wards. The blind lawyer Chen Guangcheng, who campaigned against abuses of the one-child policy, including forced abortions, was put under house arrest, then jailed, then returned to house arrest and beaten before escaping to the United States in 2012. Those regarded as trouble-makers are sent without trial to one of the PRC's 350 'reform through labour' camps; originally set up in Mao's 'anti-rightist' campaign in 1957, these jails contained some 60,000 people six decades later. A group of women who petitioned against forced abortion under the one-child policy told *Le Monde* in 2013 of one camp in northeast China where they were subjected to torture and forced to work for up to 15 hours a day, paid 5 to 25 yuan (82 cents to $4.10) a month for making jackets for companies in Australia and Italy, shirts for South Korea, and trousers for the PLA.[4]

Recurrent ideological propaganda campaigns extoll the Party as the only instrument that can make China great and ensure stability, national unity and material progress. Along with such bombast there are constant warnings about nefarious foreign activity. The ideological journal *Red Flag* warned in 2013 that 'Western nations are plotting to sink the "Great Ship" using the Internet to bring about the collapse of China.'[5] Academics in tune with the new administration and Party newspaper denounce the idea of 'constitutionalism', the school of thought that calls for the actual applications of freedoms guaranteed by the PRC's founding document, as nothing but an 'old Western' tool of oppression which can bring only chaos. Concepts such as the separation of powers are held to be alien and unsuited to China. Local officials were instructed in 2013 to 'understand the dangers posed by views and theories advocated by the West'. In an effort to 'seize control of the lectern', the new administration told university teachers to steer clear of seven taboo subjects, including universal values, judicial independence, citizens' rights and freedom of information.

This attachment to ideological ballast has its roots in the heritage of the imperial centuries. The central power believes it is the fount of all wisdom, and that, if this is questioned, the whole semi-divine system risks crashing to earth as shown by Mikhail Gorbachev's experiment with liberalization in the

USSR. This fits with the Chinese tradition, which has little or no place for incremental adaptation of the system. The country has never known a peaceful regime change; it is a matter of all or nothing: revolts, civil wars, invasions, violence: far from what admirers praise as China's innate virtues of reason.

After six decades of Communist rule, it is perfectly true that the nature of the system in the PRC makes change extremely difficult. The Party, with its 80 million members, dominates like no political movement in the West. That may be a source of admiration for some observers, but, as we will see, it brings with it systemic weakness which grows in scope as China develops, and is the biggest bar to the PRC dominating the world.

The seven-man – all its members are male – Standing Committee of the Party's Political Bureau (Politburo) sits at the apex of power. Around it are the wider, 25-person Politburo – currently including two women – and the Party Central Committee with 200 full members and 170 non-voting alternates. The Prime Minister belongs to the Standing Committee – the current incumbent ranks second to Xi Jinping. But government ministers generally have less clout than Party figures in a system that is replicated through provinces down to local level.

The Party runs its own Disciplinary Commission operating independently of the law and taking precedence. When senior politicians or officials fall from favour, they are investigated in the first instance by the Commission, which decides whether to recommend their expulsion from the Party; only then are they handed to the justice system for trial. There are Communist cells in every state agency, from the central bank to local planning authorities, and in all companies of any size. Visiting the headquarters of the big search engine Baidu in 2013, Zhao Leji, head of the Organization Department of the Party's Central Committee, said corporate cultures should be 'consistent with socialist core values'.[6] The Party is present in sports organizations, charities and entertainment troupes. As a professor told the author Richard McGregor, it is like God: everywhere but you just can't see it.[7] The regime's main newspaper, the *People's Daily*, compares the 'sacred Party spirit' to 'a Christian's belief in God'. The Party's achievement in 'leading the Chinese people to build a new China is no less than Moses leading the Israelites out of Egypt', it added.[8]

To start to dismantle or re-orientate this enormous apparatus would be a daunting task in itself. At the time of the leadership transition in 2012, as noted earlier, Wang Qishan, who was promoted to the Standing Committee at the Congress, circulated a reading list to his colleagues on which one prominent entry was Alex de Tocqueville's analysis of the fall of the Bourbon monarchy in France. The reasons the Frenchman gave for the fragility of autocracies and his observations of the dangers of ill-executed reforms have a self-evident relevance to the men running today's China.

Many of those who would have to accept change have a strong interest in maintaining the status quo. This is not simply a matter of politicians retaining power, given the Party's extensive reach and the power elite it has bred. State enterprises are integral to the system and their bosses have considerable political clout as they move between business and government in the PRC's nomenklatura. Relatives of powerful figures enjoy promotion and wealth. Even private companies often depend on their links with the Party and state, their senior executives sitting in the central or provincial legislatures.

Politicians everywhere covet power, of course, as do their parties and their business connections. What marks China is the way in which the elite sees itself as having an unquestionable grip on authority, allowing no opposition or prospect of change. That is not the case in Western democracies, Japan or Brazil, where there is debate and dialogue, however flawed and influenced by money, sectarianism or prejudice. The democratic system enables peaceful change; indeed, in some democracies, frequent change has become an integral part of the process, sometimes with disruptive effects. In the PRC, no alternative is allowed to emerge. The need to show the wisdom and unity of the Party is held to be paramount, whatever differences may exist behind the scenes. Take, for instance, the case of Bo Xilai.

Like Xi, Bo is the son of a leading Mao-era minister who was purged – with extreme violence – during the Cultural Revolution but returned to favour under Deng Xiaoping and became one of the venerated 'Eight Immortals' of the Communist Party. There were reports that, as a Red Guard, the son had denounced his father, before, like Xi, being 'sent down' to the countryside to live a menial existence. Again like Xi, he then rose through the system to hold significant posts in the northeast and became Commerce Minister after China entered the World Trade Organization at the beginning of this century. He was appointed to join the Politburo and sent in 2007 to run the mega-municipality of Chongqing, with its 32 million inhabitants and its role as spearhead of the development of western China. Some saw this as a demotion, but Bo made the post into the springboard for an unusually personalized campaign based on nostalgic appeals to the supposedly stronger and purer China of Mao Zedong. This included getting crowds to sing 'red songs' and championing state-led expansion on a massive scale – while also welcoming big foreign manufacturers to Chongqing. His fellow 'princeling' Xi Jinping was among those who paid a visit to the southwestern city to laud Bo's efforts and his highly publicized crusade against the city's underworld.

The charismatic, media-friendly Bo was aiming to get into the Politburo Standing Committee at the Party Congress in 2012, and it was widely believed that the portfolio he wanted was the one for internal security held by his hardline ally Zhou Yongkang. He enjoyed the support of leftist neo-Maoist thinkers and had links with some of the younger PLA generals. Rallies he held in Chongqing and elsewhere showed his abilities as a crowd-pleaser as he demonstrated how populist politics could be used to chart a path of quasi-autonomy from the central political machine. In the year of the Congress, it was clearly time for his colleagues to get rid of this dangerous maverick. So he was brought down as the result of a murky affair of the death of an English businessman, Neil Heywood, with whom his wife had been involved, and the attempted defection to the United States of the former police chief of Chongqing, Wang Lijun, a long-time Bo acolyte who had been rejected by his boss for unknown reasons. The politician's wife was given a suspended death sentence for allegedly poisoning Heywood after getting him drunk. Wang was convicted of treason but was sent to jail rather than being executed because of useful information he had given the prosecutors. Bo himself was expelled from the Party and held awaiting trial for what the Politburo described as 'multiple crimes', including major corruption and extra-marital affairs.

The scandal made great media and website copy inside and outside China but was, at heart, a power struggle. For the Party to get suddenly censorious about Bo's corruption stretching back for a couple of decades was hardly convincing. Nor were the affairs anything out of the ordinary: mistresses invariably figure in Chinese corruption cases – one official netted in Guangdong was said to have had 47. Bo's sin had been to seek to establish an independent power centre from which he could put pressure on the incoming leadership. Such mavericks can go only so far before the centre brings them down, as happened when Hu Jintao and Wen Jiabao toppled the Party Secretary of Shanghai, Chen Liangyu, in 2007 for operating outside central control – Chen got an 18-year prison sentence for corruption. After a trial at which he put up a spirited defence and described his wife as mentally unstable, Bo was sentenced to life imprisonment in September 2013 for taking bribes and abuse of power. He vowed to return, but this seems unlikely.

Top-level politics can thus get messy, far from the supposedly smooth mandarinate of those who trumpet the PRC as a sophisticated meritocracy. Bo's fall was followed by a campaign in the Party and the armed forces to put a lid on the case, which led to suspicions that his support had been wider than might have been expected. The five-yearly Party Congress held in November 2012 saw a series of manoeuvres and blocking moves involving past leaders, notably the former Party Chief Jiang Zemin, and the unexplained disappearance of Xi Jinping from public view for two weeks while the final shape of the transition was hammered out. The appointment of overt reformers to the Politburo Standing Committee was blocked. Their leading spokesman, Wang Yang, had been a prominent critic of Bo, and his promotion would have been too much of a victory for the reform camp on top of the defenestration of the former boss of Chongqing. In addition, Wang was thought to have spoken out too much and so had to be content with a vice premiership rather than a seat at the top Party table. The leading economic expert was moved to head a Party anti-corruption drive in part because the new Prime Minister would have found him too powerful a colleague in the government formed the following March.

Analysts like to depict the leadership as being divided between, on the one hand, the elite 'princeling' children of first-generation leaders headed by Xi Jinping and backed by Jiang Zemin and, on the other, the more populist Youth League Faction of Hu Jintao, with the new Prime Minister, Li Keqiang, as its most prominent fifth-generation member. But loyalties are much more complex. Teacher–pupil, patron–client relations redolent of the old mandarinate suffuse the system. Consensus at the summit was the hallmark of the Hu Jintao era. Xi Jinping arrived with a stronger hand to play, and set about consolidating his position – as well as drawing on the popular appeal of his wife, a well-known singer with the army entertainment corps who cut a fashionable dash, in striking contrast to the reserve of previous first ladies. But his career record and his lauding of the Mao years as well as the reform era suggest a man who still puts a premium on unquestioning unity around the ruling political party, with its inhibiting effects shown so clearly by the recourse to the lowest common denominator of agreement that has marked decision-making so far this century.

The combination of these factors prevents China going through a process of political evolution to match the growth of the economy and the changes in society. This is underpinned by a further issue, which can be summarized as follows: why should China change? Has it not achieved so much for its citizens under Communist rule that it would be folly to alter course? As Xi says repeatedly, the PRC must be true to its past, both Maoist and Dengist. The danger of this is that adherence to tradition becomes stultifying, strengthening the vested interests built up over more than 60 years and preventing the change China needs. The longer this immobility persists, the more difficult reform is rendered through the accretion of power by the status quo and the attractions of continuing as before. Deng could push through his economic revolution because the old ways had lost credibility and there was a hunger for experimentation of a different kind from Mao's adventurism – indeed there was a hunger to get away from the traumas of the previous decades and to introduce a human element into the story of Communist China. Now, in contrast, the new leader proclaims the importance of recognizing the contribution of the first three decades of Communist rule to the country's renaissance.

The next two chapters will analyse the growing challenges facing China economically and socially. But in the system installed since 1949, it is the politics that count most, and they come with a heavy historical inheritance coloured by the extraordinary ups-and-downs experienced by many of the top leaders of the People's Republic, from Mao and his colleagues through to the 'sent down' Xi Jinping. As we have seen, the launch of economic reform and opening up by Deng Xiaoping was, at base, a political calculation aimed at preserving one-party rule. The brutal suppression of the 1989 protests centred on Tiananmen Square in Beijing (though the repression stretched far beyond the square and to other cities across the PRC) was only the most naked instance of the use of violence to preserve the system. Though Deng re-launched economic reform through market mechanisms in 1992 after a temporary withdrawal and a brief conservative hiatus, his basic purpose was always clear and his ruthlessness was never in doubt.

Deng was, after all, a man who had taken a particularly harsh line against landlords in the southwest after the Communist victory and then implemented the 'anti-rightist' campaign in the mid-1950s following the brief liberalization of the Hundred Flowers episode. (Under this initiative from Mao, criticism of the regime was permitted until it became too embarrassing. The subsequent explanation was that the whole thing had been an artful exercise by the Chairman to get the 'snakes to put their heads out of their holes' so that they could be identified and suppressed.) Though Deng can have had no doubt about the disastrous nature of the Great Leap Forward launched at the end of the 1950s, he did not join another old Party comrade, Peng Dehuai, in confronting the leader, staying away from a crucial meeting on the grounds that he had broken his leg while playing billiards. Despite having been purged twice during the Cultural Revolution, he remained true to the Party he had joined as a teenager.

His belief in Communism was no doubt genuine, though he was primarily a practical operator, crossing the river by feeling the stones underfoot. But his career before the Tiananmen massacre, including the suppression of the Democracy Wall dissidents in 1979 and the jailing for 15 years of its leading figure, Wei Jingsheng, showed, above all, Deng as a believer in force to assert political power.

Once that force had been asserted, there was no reason to question why it had been required. This is a regime whose self-protectiveness borders on paranoia bred by decades of fighting for survival followed by the traumas of Mao's erratic dictatorship and his recurrent purges. Enemies were always there if they needed to be invoked, as in the case of 1989 'black hands' and foreign agents who were held to have exploited the student protests to try to bring down the socialist system and install a bourgeois republic as the vassal of the West. From this it was a straight course to buttressing the existing system with no questions asked. 'What should we do from now on?' the paramount leader asked after the repression of 1989. 'We should continue to follow unswervingly the basic line, principles and policies we have formulated.' A quarter of a century later, Tiananmen Square and the more bloody killing of citizens on the road leading into the centre of the capital remain a taboo subject.

In his remarks to the press after becoming General Secretary at the end of 2012, Xi Jinping defined the Party's role as being to rally the nation 'in taking over the relay baton passed on to us by history, and in making continued efforts to achieve the great renewal of the Chinese nation, make the Chinese nation stand rock-firm in the family of nations, and make even greater contribution to mankind'. But, like a mid-dynasty emperor facing reality, he went on to acknowledge that 'under the new conditions, our Party faces many severe challenges, and there are also many pressing problems within the Party that need to be resolved, particularly corruption, being divorced from the people, going through formalities and bureaucratism caused by some Party officials'.

The Chinese people, he said,

> wish to have better education, more stable jobs, more income, greater social security, better medical and health care, improved housing conditions, and a better environment. They want their children to have sound growth, have good jobs and lead a more enjoyable life. ... Our responsibility is weightier than Mount Tai, and our road ahead is a long one. We must always be of the same mind with the people and share the same destiny with them, and we must work together with them and diligently for the public good so as to live up to the expectations of both history and the people.

This all made eminent sense, though there is a basic paradox. Polls show high levels of public support for the regime; yet there is an evident lack of faith in the system on top of which the leaders sit, as we will see in Chapter 4. There is a sentiment, akin to that of imperial days, that the far-off rulers in Beijing are benevolent figures who would put right the misdemeanours of local officials if only they knew the truth. Like the grasping, corrupt imperial magistrates, it is the bureaucrats with whom people come into contact in their everyday lives who are seen as the villains. One major question running through this book is whether that verdict will remain in place as problems such as pollution and food safety take on ever-growing importance and people start to ask why the system as a whole cannot provide them with the protection that should be expected from a government.

Much of the loyalty the regime commands comes down to the contrast with the past – both the Mao era and the century which preceded it, during which China went through the worst protracted tribulations of any nation on earth. For the average inhabitant of the world's most populous nation, this is probably the best time to be Chinese. But satisfaction is largely predicated on the delivery of crude material progress, which could now become less of a trump card as growth slows and social tensions rise.

The wealth gap leaves many, many millions resentful; while the poor have become less poor during the era of economic growth, the rich have grown even richer. For the first decade of this century, the government did not publish the Gini coefficient measuring inequality, presumably because of the embarrassment and outrage it would have caused. When it was finally put out at the end of 2011, it was officially recorded at 0.45, with 0 representing absolute equality and 1 absolute inequality, below South Africa and Brazil but well ahead of the United States, Britain, India and Japan. A separate report by Chengdu University placed the figure for 2010 at 0.61 and evaluated the combined income of households in the rich eastern provinces to be 2.7 times that of the west and the central regions, with 10 per cent of households holding up to 57 per cent of all disposable income.[9]

Then a survey by Peking University reported that, in 2012, the richest 5 per cent earned 23 per cent of China's total household income and those in the lowest 5 per cent 0.1 per cent of total income. Average annual income for urban families was 60 per cent higher than in rural areas. The regional difference round the national mean of Rmb13,000 ($2,100, £1,390) was shown by the gap between Shanghai – just over Rmb29,000 ($4,700, £3,100) – and Gansu Province, deep inland in the northwest – Rmb11,400 ($2,000, £1,200).[10]

Xi's lists of the challenges facing the Party and of popular expectations were clear enough. In a less concentrated political system, some could be dealt with by the institutions of civil society, but, in the PRC, everything leads to the central organ of control. This is becoming a weakness which will hobble China but which, given the nature of the Party, may be beyond remedy.

Xi's initial reaction was to launch a crusade against corruption and instructions to officials to live more frugal lives. State media reported that some two thousand people were convicted on graft charges in the first three months of 2013. Bureaucrats were instructed to stop holding banquets and to content themselves with 'four dishes and a soup'. Local authorities were told to stop erecting 'glitzy' buildings. Motorcades were to cease. Xi called for a 'thorough clean-up' to get rid of 'formalism, bureaucratism, hedonism and extravagance' and to return to the 'mass line' originally urged by Mao to get the Party closer to the people. The resulting caution hit sales of Swiss watches and up-market liquor but, more seriously, slowed down the economy given the fear of being caught out in bribery integral to much of the way business is done.

Even here, the limits of the campaign were soon evident. The highest figures targeted for investigation in the first half of 2013 were one of 10 deputy directors of the national planning agency, a retired senior executive at the Agricultural Bank and a deputy Party Secretary in Sichuan Province. When the net widened in the autumn to big oil companies, the motivation was primarily political. Reports by Bloomberg and the *New York Times* of the riches amassed by relatives of Xi Jinping and Wen Jiabao led to the Internet services of those two organizations being blocked in China. Officials are reported to have become more discreet but not to have changed behaviour completely: they are careful not to wear expensive watches in public, even if the sunburn line on their wrists gives the game away. Anti-corruption campaigners who called for disclosure of assets by officials were detained.

The basic issue is one of embedded control, which the regime has pursued since 1949, but which is increasingly difficult to enforce in a rapidly evolving society with a myriad of sectional and regional elements and powerful vested interests. The model which took shape under Deng no longer reaps the dividends of the first stage of development but is producing a fast-evolving, increasingly independent-minded society out of kilter with the official mantras and the Party's proclamation of itself as the sole vanguard for the people of China.

Though so many things have changed, the Party State has not wished – or been able – to adapt its top-down approach to power. Democracy is not an immediate option. The essential underpinnings are absent, not least the rule of law, which has been overwhelmed by legalist heavy-handedness dating from the First Emperor. Yet the core equation is coming to the end of its useful life not only economically but also politically. The system implemented by Mao, continued by Deng and taken up by their successors is increasingly in conflict with the way China is evolving. To maintain the momentum essential for the system requires change. As Prime Minister Wen Jiabao put it, 'Without the success of political structural reforms, economic structural reforms cannot be carried out in full, and whatever gains we have made may be lost.' However, the ability to think out of the Mao–Deng box has become ever more limited after a decade of inertia under Hu and Wen. Xi's insistence that the PRC's history is a continuum and that the greatest priority is the preservation of Party power brings with it the danger that maintaining the status quo will be rated more important than the necessary maturing of the nation, holding back its evolution in the straitjacket imposed by the ruling political movement.

3

Inflection Point

It was in 2007 that Wen Jiabao unveiled his 'four uns'. China's economy, he said as he ended his first five years as Prime Minister, was unsustainable, uncoordinated, unbalanced, and unstable. This may have seemed strange to those who regard China's trajectory as one of virtually unalloyed success which has enabled it to take the second slot globally with $3.4 trillion in foreign exchange reserves, a low fiscal deficit and growth rates that put other major economies to shame. But the Prime Minister repeated the warning in terms which left no doubt about his awareness of the problems facing what appeared to be the world's most successful major economy. However, nothing happened as the Party establishment weighed in to block reform and the reaction of Wen's own government to the downturn at the end of 2008 repeated old policies that made things worse. As he and Hu Jintao stepped down in 2012–13, their 10 years in office looked like a lost decade when it came to adapting the PRC to the more testing environment that loomed in the second decade of the 21st century.

Still, Wen's successor, Li Keqiang, who has a doctorate in economics, took up the baton. He gave his approval to a report issued in early 2012 by a group set up by the State Council and the World Bank which called for the PRC to 'complete its transition to a market economy – through enterprise, land, labour, and financial sector reforms – strengthen its private sector, open its markets to greater competition and innovation, and ensure equality of opportunity to help achieve its goal of a new structure for economic growth'. It proposed to dismantle the state monopolies in key sectors and to raise productivity.[1]

After becoming Prime Minister in March 2013, Li made statements pledging 'an all-round effort to deepen market-oriented reform, unleash the dividends of change, and continue to grow the economy, improving livelihoods and promoting social equity'. He spoke of carrying out a 'self-imposed revolution' in the economy. 'All of society is ardently awaiting new breakthroughs in reform,' a government directive declared. Li even spoke of potential pain as China went into cold turkey to shed its high growth habit.[2]

Given China's economic achievements, the question might be asked: "What needs to be changed after such a successful record? For an answer, turn to Wen's 'four uns'.

(1) **The economy is unsustainable**. Industrialization since the 1980s has neglected fundamental long-term issues in favour of short-term results – in sharp contrast to the image of the PRC as the home of efficient, long-term planning. The system promoted by the ruling caste has promoted many of these fault lines, including an enormous environmental crisis that will be described in the next chapter. In contrast to the picture of China bestriding the world economically, the country remains dependent on raw materials from abroad, with food likely to join hard commodities as a major import.

Agriculture meets food demand only thanks to a string of good harvests. Water is in short supply in northern China – the future Prime Minister, Wen Jiabao, warned in 1999 that the shortage threatened the survival of the nation.[3] But the low controlled price levels encourage wastage. Little has been done to check the potential disastrous shortfall in northern wheat-growing regions as urban demand has rocketed owing to the expansion of Beijing, Tianjin and other big cities. Desalination is at an early stage and its costs are higher than the average selling price. The south–north water diversion project begun in 2002 is planned to pump 45 billion cubic metres a year from the Yangtze and its tributaries, but it is not due for completion until the middle of this century and there is no telling the impact on the level or quality of rivers and their eco-systems. There is a vicious circle between two resources of which China is short, water and energy; development of shale gas and nuclear power to help meet energy demand is constrained by a shortage of the water needed in both processes, while desalination uses a lot of energy on which China is trying to economize.

Urbanization has boosted the proportion of city residents from 18 to 53 per cent of the population since 1980 and is expected to reach 70 per cent by 2030 with an annual influx of 15–20 million from the countryside. But it has been pursued with scant attention to developing sustainable, liveable cities, and the numbers mean more than two hundred centres with more than a million residents by 2030, with all the attendant strains this will bring.

(2) **The economy is uncoordinated.** Growth has come from exports and fixed asset investment in construction and infrastructure. Consumption

plays a much smaller role and has fallen as a proportion of GDP this century – overall consumption accounts for just 50 per cent of GDP and household consumption for only 35 per cent, far below the global average. The services sector fell behind (from an already low base) as manufacturing boomed. Capital took the lion's share of economic expansion while wages represented a far lower slice of national income, an irony in a supposedly Communist state. With low interest rates, households got small returns on their savings, which were channelled to fund projects in what is known as financial repression – taking the money of the people to fund the state and its elite of government bodies, companies and individuals.

The result was an unhealthy reliance on more and more construction to keep up the GDP figures, with major misallocation of capital and a declining rate of return on projects approved by officials whose promotion prospects are boosted by delivering crude growth numbers. At the same time, the way most tax revenue goes to the central government means local authorities are short of cash to meet spending obligations; to fill the gap, they requisition farm land, classify it for development and sell it to developers, with social consequences we will see in the next chapter.

The Five-Year Plan for 2011–15 provided for rebalancing from investment and exports to consumption and services. Sales abroad did, indeed, fall, with the trade surplus component of GDP dropping from 10 per cent in 2007 to 2.6 per cent in 2012 as the world economy slowed after the financial crisis. But investment rose as a share of GDP in 2012 while that of household consumption declined. Services edged up by only 1.4 per cent between 2010 and 2012. The reason was simple: for all Wen Jiabao's fine talk of the need to shift the economy, his bigger concern was to maintain growth, which meant falling back on the short-term recipe of pumping more cash into infrastructure projects and maintaining property construction.

(3) **The economy is unbalanced**. Alongside the mismatch between investment and consumption, development has been largely concentrated in coastal areas following the initial 'Special Economic Zones' (SEZs) set up under Deng to spearhead growth. Inland China fell behind, especially the countryside, which constitutes most of the country's landmass. A report by Chengdu University for 2010 found that the combined income of households in eastern provinces was 2.7 times that of the west and the central regions. Deprived of rights in

the places where they work, migrant workers form an underclass of more than 150 million.

While China is indeed set to overtake the United States in absolute GDP size, it will lag far behind for decades in per capita terms, though, of course, a dollar or its equivalent in yuan buys far more in the PRC than it does in the United States. The International Monetary Fund's rankings of wealth per inhabitants put the PRC 86th on a nominal basis in 2012, between Iraq and Turkmenistan. A United Nations survey the previous year had it 93rd and the World Bank ranked it at 114th with gross national income per capita of $4,940. More than 150 million people live below the $1.25-a-day international poverty line. As the World Bank wrote in a report in 2012: 'With the second largest number of poor in the world after India, poverty reduction remains a fundamental challenge.' The IMF, meanwhile, noted: 'High income inequality and environmental problems are further signs that the current growth model needs to change,' saying in mid-2013 that such a shift was 'increasingly urgent'.[4]

A new imbalance is developing as the fast-growing ranks of the old outstrip the falling number of young people coming into the labour force, chipping away at the 'demographic dividend' that helped to power growth – and this in a state whose pensions system is weak and under-funded.

(4) **The economy is unstable**. These inequalities lead to discontent, augmented by an array of social factors that will be dealt with in the next chapter. But apart from 150,000 to 180,000 protests each year, the elements listed above produce an unstable economic structure which stands in sharp contrast to the progress shown in the top-line data of the past decades.

The 2008 stimulus programme is a good example of this. It was hailed by the leadership, including Wen, as a triumph which showed the PRC's ability to achieve results unattainable by the United States and Europe. The data certainly looked good: after dropping at the end of 2008, growth moved to just over 10 per cent in both 2009 and 2010. But that was achieved by a flood of cheap credit funnelled through state banks to yet more of the projects mentioned above. Some were useful but others were never going to show much of a financial or social return and were either pump-priming for the sake of the numbers or a means for officials to divert cash to their localities or their own pockets. By 2010 China was riding on a sea of liquidity. Inflation soared and local governments were saddled with debts that they could never repay. Tightening had to be brought in, slowing growth to 9.2 per cent in 2011, 7.8 per cent in 2012 and 7.5 per cent in mid-2013. Lending switched from state banks to 'shadow banking': raising money through trust companies, wealth management products and corporate bonds. As a result, the overall debt burden as a proportion of GDP in China rose by 84 per cent between 2008 and 2013, twice as much as it had done in the United States in the five years before the 2008 crisis.[5]

That switchback pattern showed a fifth 'un': uncontrolled. As he stepped down in 2001 after bringing down inflation, streamlining the state sector and ushering China into the World Trade Organization, Prime Minister Zhu Rongji proposed a target of annual growth of 7 per cent for the following five years; the actual average was 10.4 in 2003-6. The target for the Five-Year Plan for 2006-10 was 7.5 per cent for the whole period, with 8 per cent for 2007; but the final figure for that year was 13 per cent. The Five-Year Plan for 2011–15 provides for 7 per cent annual expansion in pursuit of a more sustainable economic course and rebalancing away from dependence on fixed asset investments in the shape of infrastructure and construction towards increased consumption as a driver of the economy. The number for 2011 was

9.2 per cent and, despite a significant subsequent slowdown, 2012 was still almost one point ahead of projections at 7.8 per cent.

Such numbers may delight China bulls when compared to anaemic data from developed economies, European ones in particular – though even they have started to recognize the dangers of runaway expansion. The data certainly cast considerable doubts on the ability of China's planners, who are either poor forecasters or equally poor policy enforcers – or both. The device used to take the bad loans of the big four banks off their balance sheets before they issued shares at the turn of the century is a good example of how slow progress often is; 15 years later, 60 per cent of the money advanced by the state to fund this operation remains outstanding and the recovery rate on the loans is 20 per cent. The constant rolling out of plans may appear impressive to those who dismiss the short-termism of democratic governments that have to win elections but they are, all too often, not carried out as laid down on paper, while basic questions remain over the validity of the underlying data. In part, this is because of the sheer difficulty of administering a country as large as China with a limited corps of civil servants and the age-old tension between the centre and the provinces. Tellingly, Li Keqiang, whose reservations about the figures have already been noted, felt he had to spell out in one of his early speeches as Premier that 'the central government will lead by example. Local governments must follow suit.'[6]

This flaw in what is meant to be a smooth, top-down system is greatly exacerbated by the structural weaknesses in the economy, which contribute powerfully to the 'four uns'. Headlong growth masked these flaws as the 'China model' seemed all-triumphant; now they have to be addressed if the PRC is to continue to move forward. But in each case there are powerful political and systemic forces working against the change which the leaders know is required, but from which they have shrunk for fear of weakening the regime.

Starting at the base, agriculture needs a through shake-up. All farmland belongs to the state. It is distributed to rural households on a leasehold basis – extended from 30 to 60 years in 2009 in a compromise at the end of an internal debate about whether to grant ownership rights to farmers. That was refused for three reasons: a remaining ideological argument in favour of state possession; the desire of local authorities to retain the right to requisition land to raise money; and the fear on the part of city authorities of an influx of people from the countryside who would have sold their land and moved to urban areas which could not absorb them.

The leasehold system means that Chinese farming is characterized by small plots which can support a family but do not permit more efficient, mechanized operations. The flood of migrant workers from rural areas to cities produces a shortage of people of working age who know how to farm. Education in anything but basic agricultural technology is sparse. Moreover, pollution, often carried by rivers, damages farmland, while poor-quality nitrate fertilizers leach out the soil and toxic chemical waste infects crops, including rice.

Urbanization, pollution and desertification are eating into arable land – China is on the cusp of the acreage it needs to feed itself under the government's policy of 95 per cent self-sufficiency (except for soy). The water shortage adds to the pressure in the wheat-growing regions of the north, where the aquifers are drying up and available supplies are diverted to mega-cities. The logistics of food distribution are poorly developed, with a lack of refrigerated transport and warehouses. There are some big producers of China's favourite meat, pork, but many of the animals are kept by small farmers who breed and slaughter a few pigs according to short-term market movements, producing alternate gluts and shortages that fuel inflation as the cycle turns.

As for China's vast army of migrant workers, the *hukou* household registration system means they only qualify for health, education, welfare, pension and property rights in their homeplace. This has important social repercussions, as will be laid out in the next chapter. It also constricts the labour market. As the government encourages the development of the inland areas from which most of the migrants come, companies in the coastal regions have to increase wages to attract them, boosting costs at a time when China faces growing competition from other developing nations. A survey of PRC companies by Standard Chartered Bank in 2013 showed that half had been obliged to increase wages more than they had expected in the manufacturing hub of the Pearl River as labour became scarce, with knock-on effects on inland regions.[7]

Local government finance is in a parlous state in many parts of the country, pushing provincial and sub-provincial authorities to depend on sales of land and loans to meet spending obligations. The financial sector, under the control of the state and its big banks, has been the scene of major misallocation of capital as loan policy was decided by administrative quotas, with cash going overwhelmingly to state enterprises. Financial repression of households encouraged them to go after the far greater wealth enhancement offered by property. Since private ownership of real estate was introduced at the end of the 1990s, the economy has become uncomfortably reliant on the continuing health of the residential market, with nearly 90 per cent of families fully or partially owning their homes, according to a 2013 survey by Peking University, which also found that more than 10 per cent had two or more homes.[8]

The currency and capital accounts are controlled; while there have been moves to increase international use of the yuan, real liberalization would produce a major outflow of funds from Chinese seeking to diversify their assets. As it is, transfers of money abroad, sometimes through illegal channels, are a feature of today's China, reflecting lack of confidence and a desire to build up holdings beyond the mainland.

Cheap credit from the big banks cushions inefficient state enterpises. The under-pricing of the two major inputs of which China is short, water and energy, leads to wastage on a major scale. The lack of an independent legal system, weak accountability and regulation, plus widespread corruption, mean that business is conducted on a potentially shifting basis in which the fall of a political protector can bring down a company, decision-making is opaque and dodges proliferate.

So, far from being the smoothly executing machine its admirers laud, China faces major economic challenges. These have been avoided to date by the scale of growth achieved since the launch of the Deng revolution. But that revolution remains only half accomplished. The second part is likely to be considerably more testing than the first, with the evaporation of the equation between cheap labour, cheap capital and strong export markets at the end of the global supply chain.

Like motherhood and apple pie, reform is generally regarded as being automatically a good thing. There was an assumption at the end of 2012 that the advent of new men to run China must mean new policies which would usher in a new era. We have seen how little evidence there is for this in the political sphere. As regards the economy, structural reform would reduce growth and increase inflation for several years. It would be bad for Chinese equity markets.

State-owned enterprises (SOEs), which are mainstays of the system and whose shares dominate the Shanghai and Shenzhen exchanges, ride on subsidies and preferential treatment; one study puts state assistance between 1985 and 2005 at more than $300 billion.[9] Well-connected private companies benefit, too. If reform affected this through increased input prices for energy and water and greater cost of capital, many SOEs would go into loss. As it is, the index of shares of big state companies on the Shanghai exchange fell by 40 per cent between 2009 and 2013 compared to a 1 per cent drop for private companies. The investment bank Morgan Stanley reports that the return on equity of big state enterprises dropped from 10 to 6 per cent between 2009 and 2013.[10]

If a long-dormant scheme to make SOEs pay proper dividends to their main shareholder, the state, was implemented, it could provide funding for welfare and education but would, obviously, reduce the cash the firms hold and can use to finance themselves or lend out to earn extra revenue. Effective controls on pollution would require additional spending by factories, while a more independent legal system would expose companies to greater external scrutiny and the need for more accountability. Moreover, the end of the *hukou* system would increase the bargaining power of migrant workers.

The reluctance of central and local authorities to take the risks that come with reform has exacerbated the problem. If Xi Jinping and his colleagues do have the will and ability to make the changes to propel China into a new stage of development, their task will be made that much tougher by the 'lost decade' under Hu and Wen. The lack of significant action between 2002 and 2012 (except for lifting the farm tax to help the rural world in 2005) may have been understandable politically given the boost of joining the World Trade Organization in 2001 and the exuberance that reigned as the PRC seemed to have a one-way ticket to growth and prosperity. But the story since the boom slowed down in 2008 shows that the economic model needs restructuring. The problem there is one of skills and standards.

The roadmap set in the Five-Year Plan for 2011–15 provides for industry to move up the value chain and for rebalancing towards consumption away from investment and exports as a growth driver. That is eminently sensible, but there are serious snags. The policy adopted in the summer of 2010 was to raise consumption by increasing wages, with instructions to the monopoly trade union to stop acting as an agent of management, as in the past, and to go to bat for workers. The result was substantial pay rises: the minimum wage in some industries almost doubled in four years. But demand continued to rise at roughly the previous level.

One major reason was simple: in the absence of

a proper health service, with poor public education standards and low pensions, people continue to save in case they fall ill, to pay for private education and to provide for their old age. Health insurance has been extended to 90 per cent of the population, but it provides funding for only three days in hospitals which are known to eject patients with terminal illnesses who cannot pay for treatment and which rely on sales of expensive drugs for their revenue. Other seriously ill people simply do not bother to enrol for care. A study published in 2013 reported that illness eats up 40 per cent of the annual disposable income of rural residents. If government plans for health provision are implemented, this caution will be less evident at the end of the present decade.[11] Equally, the government is committed to spend more on schools and to set up a proper pension system for the army of old people which will result from the shifting dynamics of demography (analysed in the next chapter).

But Xi and his team have to deal with the here and now at a time when the challenges are rising for the model on which China runs. Other low-cost countries are providing a growing rivalry in a world export market that is not what it was. Advances in manufacturing technology may restore an edge to developed nations. The shale gas revolution in the United States has the potential to change the balance of input costs. Meanwhile, wage rises, increased costs, the pressure of food demand and the rising price of capital are all likely to turn China from a deflationary economy into an inflationary one. The financial system is coming under strain from the huge expansion in lending as the multiplier effect of credit on growth produces diminishing results: while social financing at the start of 2013 was 63 per cent higher than in the same period of 2012, growth slowed nonetheless. As the IMF put it in measured language in 2013, the rapid expansion in funding 'raises concerns about the quality of investment and its impact on repayment capacity, especially since a fast-growing share of credit is flowing through less-well supervised parts of the financial system'.[12]

As for moving up the value chain, there are two major issues connected with this laudable goal. The first is employment. Given the popular image of China as one great workshop, it is easy to ignore the importance of jobs for the regime. George W. Bush records in his memoirs that, when he and Hu Jintao discussed what kept them awake at night, the Chinese leader said it was the need for job creation. Unemployment is certainly higher than the official figure of a little above 4 per cent – it may be double that, plus considerable underemployment particularly in rural areas and the old rust belt of the northeast – but it is not at the level that causes mass social instability. This is something the leadership has to prevent. Hence, for instance, the use of state firms to keep operating plants that retain people in work even when they are not needed, contributing, for instance, to the 30 per cent over-capacity in sectors such as steel and aluminium which produces losses and a glut of loss-making supply to export markets.

Moving up the value chain by introducing more modern technology would, however, lead to fewer jobs. Already, smaller private sector manufacturers say they are reacting to higher wages by installing more machines to take the place of human hands. If that continues, two core objectives of government and Party policy – to give China a more advanced industrial machine and to preserve jobs – must come into conflict. The only hope would lie in the decline in the number of entrants into the labour force as falling fertility and the one-child policy change the demographics. That would be a happy conjunction of circumstances but there is no guarantee it will happen – or, if it does, that it will be a smooth process.

The other big snag is the skills gap and the weakness of regulation to ensure that more advanced products are safe and properly maintained. Coal mine and factory accidents are a recurrent feature of Chinese industry, but now new problems are becoming apparent. The crash of two high-speed trains in eastern China in 2011 was a stark reminder that, while the PRC can buy or copy foreign technology, it also has to be able to operate it safely. China has few world brands with not a single entry among the top 20 for retail or the top 10 banks. It has only one company, PetroChina, among the 10 most valuable quoted enterprises in the world compared to five in 2008. Its big computer firm, Lenovo, is the result of the purchase of part of IBM's business, while its communications giant Huawei is subject to persistent questioning about its links with the state and the army.[13]

The high volume of Chinese patent applications is more the result of official encouragement to do so than of real innovation. China is, in general, good at applying the inventions of others rather than perpetuating the great innovative tradition of its distant past. While its patent office became the busiest in the world in 2011 with slightly more applications than in the United States, the vast majority involved small changes to existing products and the PRC ranked 13th in the world when it came to international patents. Very few Chinese patent applications are also lodged abroad, compared with 40 per cent of those in Europe and 27 per cent of those in America, indicating that the Chinese ones are of limited and national scope.[14]

China has enormous ecommerce companies: Alibaba operates the world's biggest online marketplace for trade between firms, for example – but most mirror originators in the United States. Huawei has developed innovative telecommunications systems that spread globally when not blocked by political fears, but progress in advanced sectors usually depends heavily on imported technology. The efficiency of SOEs is affected by their wider obligations, for instance to maintain employment, and by the way in which they form part of a politically directed system in which a top manager may be switched to run a province or assume a Party post. Foreign visitors say they meet 'some really smart' managers in the PRC; the problem is that they may be working in a business context which is often short-term or conditioned by political and other external considerations.

Li Keqiang has shown himself aware of the limits of state direction. 'If we place excessive reliance on government steering and policy leverage to stimulate growth, that will be difficult to sustain and could even produce new problems and risks,' he said after becoming Prime Minister. He stressed the need for the state to retreat in favour of the market's ability to create more evenly distributed wealth and, after taking office, proposed to reduce administrative approval procedures. At the same time, the planning agency, the National Development and Reform Commission (NDRC), laid out plans for gradual liberalization of interest rates and 'promoting the effective entry of private capital into finance, energy, railways, telecommunications and other spheres', with foreign investors gaining greater access to finance, logistics and health care. Moreover, the State-owned Assets Supervision and Administration Commission (SASAC), which oversees the biggest SOEs, told them it expects profit growth of at least 10 per cent and sent inspection teams to probe the operations of some big state groups which have not been performing well.

The intention was there, obviously, but the strength of the system makes it difficult to evolve alternative models and then to implement them against the power of vested interests. The head of SASAC was abruptly sacked and investigated for corruption in what looked like a politically motivated case in the late summer of 2013. The phrase 'trapped transition', used by the political scientist

Minxin Pei as the title of his 2008 book, risks being highly prescient. The dismantling of a command economy is by its nature a tricky process that can easily run out of control, as shown by Russia after the collapse of Communism. Absent a major crisis, the lure of going on as before is always strong.

Many of the economic challenges facing the PRC are normal for a massive, complex country like China in the fourth decade of its post-Mao development process. They in no way gainsay the progress that has been achieved, but they call for a degree of realism about China's prospects of dominating the globe given the systemic risks. In discussions with a visiting IMF team in the spring of 2013, the new authorities emphasized their intention of 'embarking on a comprehensive reform agenda to bring about more balanced, inclusive and environmentally friendly growth'. But, as the visitors noted:

> While China still has significant policy space and financial capacity to maintain stability even in the face of adverse shocks, the margins of safety are narrowing and a decisive impetus to reforms is needed to contain vulnerabilities and move the economy to a more sustainable growth path.[15]

That is made more complex by the intersection of politics and the economy which has underpinned the story so far and has been described in this and the previous chapter. That conjunction is at the core of the way China works but is put in jeopardy by the evolution of society and threats to the quality of life spawned by runaway growth, as we will now see.

4

Behind the Dream

Beside the political and economic challenges the PRC faces lies a nexus of social issues which may be the greatest test of Xi Jinping and his colleagues and of the system over which they preside. The ingredients range from wealth disparities to corruption, from the trust deficit to the impact of pollution and recurrent food safety scandals. Taken together they constitute different kinds of 'why' questions about China: Why has the priority been so overwhelmingly on building hardware rather than improving the quality of life? Why have the benefits of material progress not been shared more equitably? Why can the state, which claims such power, not guarantee such basic elements as clean water, trustworthy food and legal protection? Why is the political focus on preserving the system rather than encouraging greater public participation? Why is there so much corner-cutting and such a lack of common trust between rulers and ruled?

The Chinese may have more reverence for the state than is common in the West, but that tradition is based on the bargain that the state will act as protector, and the PRC has not been doing a great job in this respect. The regime faces no threat of being overthrown, but there is a very real danger that it may lose public respect as merely making money becomes less of a priority among the 400 million or so people whose incomes gives them time to wonder why such basic livelihood matters are not addressed more effectively, their concerns spread by social media and greater individual liberty.

Still, money remains at the core of the way China works today. There is no record of Deng Xiaoping ever having said 'it is glorious to be rich', but this became the motto of the economic revolution he launched. The PRC contains an estimated one million dollar millionaires – the numbers may actually be an under-estimate since many rich people like to keep their wealth to themselves. Conspicuous consumption is a hallmark of smart China. The Confucian disdain for money-making has little purchase on those driving the economy, producing a fundamental problem for observers who see the sage's teachings as constituting a major element in propelling the PRC to global dominance.

Materialism is the most powerful 'ism' in today's China, epitomized by the young woman who said on a television dating show that she would 'rather cry in the back of a BMW than laugh on the back of a bicycle', and by the hit 2013 film *Tiny Times* tracking the lives of four free-spending fashionable young women in Shanghai. But materialism unleashes aspirations and behaviour patterns at odds with the official ethos. Money-making breeds individualism. The human factor has thus become of greater importance than in the days when emperors or revolutionary leaders could regard the Chinese as grains of sand or numbers to be shaken about at the will of those in power.

While this is most apparent among the middle class, it is also detectable in the industrial workforce, with a rising pattern of strikes and wage pressure. The monopoly All China Trade Union Federation, which has traditionally acted as an arm of the regime and of management, is under pressure from workers who want to exercise their rights. Second-generation migrants and young women are less willing to be human components on the assembly line, bereft of rights in their adopted urban homes.

At the same time, however, people seem to be uncomfortable with the scale of inequalities spawned by the way China has grown. This is not resentment at wealth appreciation as such; rather it is a matter of unhappiness that some have used their positions or illicit methods to accumulate wealth without any control by the authorities – and with the way in which hundreds of millions have been left behind. The Pew poll in 2012 found that 87 per cent of those questioned thought the rich–poor gap was 'at least a moderately big problem' while 48 per cent saw it as 'a very serious problem' – up from 41 per cent in 2008. Eighty-one per cent agreed with the view that the 'rich just get richer while the poor get poorer'.

This is one of a raft of concerns Chinese express to poll-takers and which seem, at first sight, to contradict the high levels of approval for their country's economic progress and the performance of the central government. What we have here is top-line satisfaction with the way the PRC has evolved in the last three decades, but, below this, a range of everyday complaints on specific issues such as land requisitioning by local government without adequate compensation, police misbehaviour, corruption and pollution. Local officials get low ratings in keeping with the way in which, in

imperial times, people complained about oppres-
sive, grasping local magistrates while venerating the
man on the Dragon Throne. Petitioners still travel
to Beijing during the annual plenary session of the
legislature to try to get satisfaction, even if they are
often rounded up by thugs, put into 'black jails' and
shipped back home.

A Gallup poll conducted in 155 countries between
2005 and 2009 to measure satisfaction and happiness levels placed the PRC in 125th place globally.
A survey in Party media in 2010 reported that 73.5
per cent of respondents felt 'vulnerable' – nearly
half the officials questioned put themselves in that
category. The high ratio of property prices to
incomes produces constant stress for urban residents on the lower rungs of the real estate ladder in
a society where owning your home is an essential
mark of success.

The Blue Book of China's Society for 2011, com-
piled by the Chinese Academy of Social Sciences,
reported declining levels of job satisfaction and
falling confidence in social welfare. The White
Book of Happiness of Middle-Class Families, which
surveyed 100,000 people from 35 cities, found that
more than half those questioned said they were not
happy. A questionnaire in late 2009 asked academics, Communist Party cadres and the general public

to name the biggest problems China would face in the coming decade. Corruption and the wealth divide headed the responses, followed by 'a crisis of trust and loss of moral standards'. When the Party newspaper, *People's Daily*, opened an on-line poll on Xi Jinping's China Dream, 70 per cent swiftly expressed disapproval, and the site was closed.

Any one survey may be questioned, but such a mass of evidence points to problems at the heart of the People's Republic and where it is headed which reach beyond conventional politics and economics and look like blind-siding the regime's levers of power and authority.

To start with, China is on the edge of a demographic crisis. The one-child policy, which affects only around 65 per cent of the population, is not the only factor. Fertility has been falling since the early 1970s and contraception has become more common. It is also increasingly expensive to have and to raise children. Average births per woman are 1.6 in the PRC, 2.1 in the United States and 2.7 in India. The Health Ministry says doctors have performed more than 330 million abortions since 1971.

In 2012, the size of the working population fell for the first time under Communist rule as China reached the Lewis Turning Point where the 'demographic dividend' starts to erode. Forecasts of the drop in the number of people aged between 15 and 64 range around 40 million between 2014 and 2030. Meanwhile, improved health care swells the ranks of the elderly; life expectancy has risen to an average of 73.5 years. The number of people aged over 60 in 2013 stood at 185 million, or 15 per cent of the population, and will go to 487 million by 2053 according to the China National Committee on Ageing.[1] While the United States and India grow younger, China may become old before it gets rich as its younger generation grapples with the 1:2:4 ratio by which each worker has to support two parents and four grandparents.[2]

Nearly a quarter of the elderly are below the poverty line. The pension system covers only about 20 per cent of living expenses. Beijing has only three beds in social welfare homes for every 100 old people. The impact of weak health provision is felt most by the old. Polls report 40 per cent of elderly people living in cities saying that they suffer from depression. Family cohesion seems to be fraying: one study showed almost half China's old folk living alone or with their grandchildren.[3]

Rural China is full of villages populated by the elderly or infants, the rest of the original inhabitants having gone to work in cities. A survey in

Guangdong showed that a quarter of old people received only one visit a year from their children; three-quarters of those questioned said they longed for more moral support from their offspring. A law was introduced in 2013 ordering children to visit their parents and 'never neglect or snub elderly people'. What does the need for legislation say about the piety towards elders supposedly inherent in China's civilization?

With the demographic shift, China has acquired a serious gender imbalance as parents abort female foetuses or abandon female babies. Males are regarded as being more likely to be able to support their parents and they alone can pay homage to ancestors and ensure that the family lineage is preserved. The male:female ratio at birth has widened from 108.5:100 in 1982 to 120:100 in 2013 – the shortage of young women of marriageable age has led to what is known as the 'bride price' in the form of a lavish dowry from the groom. Such 'male bulges' have been linked by some historians to imperial expansion by European powers after 1500 and Japan after 1914. So we have the prospect of a China powered by a testosterone rush, coming at a time when the growth of universities has resulted in millions of unemployed but educated young men.

Environmental damage has reached crisis point

in some parts of China and is dragging down GDP growth. Though there are strict ecological protection laws, they are poorly implemented. Environment Ministry offices across the country are part of local governments which may have interests in polluting factories. A coal power plant opens on average every 10 days. Sulphur from diesel trucks is more than 20 times the level in the West. Serious air pollution – the airpocalypse – regularly envelops Beijing and other major cities in northern China with toxic smog containing particulate matter 40 times the maximum level regarded as safe by the World Health Organization. While the government has announced major initiatives to try to clean things up, outdoor air pollution is estimated to contribute to 1.2 million premature deaths a year, and a study published in 2013 found that it reduced the life expectancy of inhabitants of northern cities by 5.5 years.[4] That is without taking into account heavy cigarette smoking, which kills 2,000 people a day and could produce an annual death toll of 2 million by 2025. [5]

Water quality is low owing to industrial waste and the flow of fertilizers and pesticides from fields. There are some 10,000 petrochemical plants along the Yangtze and 4,000 on the Yellow River, neither of which is the most polluted of China's waterways.

Up to half China's rivers were reported seriously polluted in 2012, with anywhere from 20 to 40 per cent so toxic that contact was dangerous. A quarter of 60 lakes and reservoirs have excessive amounts of algae. Waste disposal has seriously affected the sea off the PRC. A 2012 report by the Land Ministry found that of 4,929 groundwater monitoring sites across the country, 41 per cent had poor water quality and almost 17 per cent had extremely poor water quality containing levels of iron, manganese, fluoride, nitrites, nitrates, ammonium and heavy metals exceeding safe limits.[6] The resulting annual human toll is put at 60,000 premature deaths.

The Three Gorges Dam, touted as the biggest project on earth when completed in 2006, is subject to major questioning – over its cost, the 1.3 million people displaced from their homes, its effect on the flow of the Yangtze river and downstream farming, and the creation of what one monitoring group calls 'a festering bog of effluent, silt, industrial pollutants and rubbish' stretching for more than a hundred miles up-river.[7] Heavy metal discharges from smelters and factories cause cancer and dangerously high levels of lead in blood. Pollution is the main cause of the doubling of the birth-defect rate in Beijing in the last 10 years. The number of asbestos-related deaths is put at anywhere from 15,000 to 40,000 a year. Solar panel manufacturing has produced lakes of toxic slurry. Recycling of electronic parts imported from the rich world has created villages surrounded by a wasteland of corroded circuit boards, mobile telephone cases and graphic cards stripped of their chips.[8]

Lack of food safety is a recurrent cause for concern. Milk is laced with the dangerous chemical melamine to boost its protein count. In 2008, contaminated baby formula affected 300,000 children, of whom 54,000 were treated in hospital and six died – similar cases have surfaced subsequently. Parents who can afford to do so stock up on milk powder for their young infants when they travel outside the mainland; so much so that Hong Kong introduced rationing of such products in 2013.

Putrid meat is sold after being treated with chemicals. A major processing firm was forced to admit in 2011 that a subsidiary had used pork from pigs fed with the growth enhancer clenbuterol, which can cause serious illness in humans (its use was subsequently banned). Two years later, more than 16,000 carcasses of diseased pigs floated down the river through Shanghai from farms in Zhejiang Province while, elsewhere in the same region, rat meat was dressed up to be sold as mutton. An outbreak of drug-resistant bird flu killed 36 people in the first half of 2013. A big-selling brand of bottled water, meanwhile, was found to have arsenic levels far beyond benchmark safety standards. Even China's staple food is not immune from contamination. As a result of industrial waste and poor quality fertilizers, the Food and Drug Administration in the huge southern city of Guangzhou reported in 2013 that 44 per cent of rice samples contained dangerously high amounts of cadmium, which can cause cancer and kidney failure. Researchers in Nanjing said that 10 per cent of the national rice crop is contaminated.[9]

China's safety fault-lines stretch from toys containing lead paint to transport. The nuclear industry has only a fraction of the supervisory staff it needs if expansion plans are realized. An investigation of Chinese airlines in 2010 found that they employed more than 200 pilots with fake qualifications. More than 2,000 coal miners die underground each year; in the spring of 2013, 83 copper miners were killed in a landslide in Tibet amid allegations of lack of safety precautions. That May, a fire in a poultry slaughterhouse in northern China killed 119 people inside, largely because the doors had been locked from the outside to prevent them leaving their work stations during their shifts.

There is a serious shortage of qualified managers.

John Quelch, former Dean of the London Business School, who was appointed to head the China Europe International Business School in Shanghai, speaks of 'a certain undercurrent of Chinese exceptionalism, with managers thinking themselves brilliant – "We know better and we can do everything." This can lead to risky hubris.'[10] That is a sobering observation at a time when the PRC wants to move up the technological chain with a need to supervise complex industrial systems. The high-speed train crash in eastern China in 2011 was such a shock because it punctured the idea that the PRC could do anything it liked faster and bigger than any other nation and exposed the management weaknesses in the runaway rail project.

Similar problems were certainly present in now-developed nations as they grew. But they take on an acute character in today's China precisely because of its global importance and what they say about national priorities. The PRC can put on the mega-show of the 2008 Olympics and build a high-speed train network from nothing, airports that put the rest of the world to shame, multi-lane highways and forests of tower blocks. But its pollution gets worse and worse, and regulation remains weak, whatever the rules say and despite budgeted spending of $375 billion on environmental protection and energy conservation between 2010 and 2015.

All too often, the lack of care is buttressed by political protection for offenders and the official obsession with control. Despite all the pollution of farmland, which is estimated to affect anywhere from 8 to 20 per cent of arable acreage,[11] soil content is a state secret. Courts are weak and may declare themselves unqualified to deal with cases where local interests are the defendants. For factory owners, paying the low fines is cheaper than installing clean equipment. Knowing that their career prospects are tied to the economic growth they deliver, local officials have allowed polluting factories to get away with it so long as they boost GDP numbers.

Such weaknesses have been underpinned by corruption, which has been estimated to amount to 3 per cent of GDP[12] and leads to misallocation of resources, the skirting of regulations, the exploitation of those unable to join in the graft game, and deep public cynicism. China fell from 85th to 90th place in the annual rankings by the anti-graft body Transparency International in 2012. Big cases grab headlines when they are exposed, but graft is endemic throughout the system as money is diverted from its intended destination to enrich officials. The

2008 earthquake in Sichuan killed 5,000 children in schools which had been poorly built as functionaries squirrelled away the cash. Contractors bidding for public works projects regularly include a provision for bribes in their calculations. A prominent property developer complains that if one gets rich in China it is assumed that one must be corrupt.

Or, at a mundane level, take the case of a Beijing private school where the principal insisted on having an unnecessary ornate gateway built instead of buying much-needed gymnasium equipment and musical instruments. A mother with a child at the school smiles as she says she understands that the school head can expect under-the-counter payments from construction companies but not from sellers of vaulting horses or violins. When a reporter for *Southern Metropolitan News* asked primary school pupils what they wanted to be when they grew up, most gave the usual reply of sports star, rich business person or famous performer. One girl said she would like to be an official. What kind of official, the reporter asked. A corrupt official because they have all the nice things, came the reply.[13]

The Railways Minister, Liu Zhijun, who ran the high-speed rail programme which involved spending of Rmb1.98 trillion (US$320 billion) until he was brought down in 2011 (before the crash), was handed a suspended death sentence for raking in Rmb64.6 million, while media reports said a businesswoman who acted as go-between with major firms netted Rmb2.4 billion (US$390 million); she also supplied him with mistresses and helped get lenient treatment for his brother when he was accused of plotting the murder of a rival.

After reaching the very top, Xi Jinping recognized the scale of the problem by launching a crusade against corruption spearheaded by Politburo Standing Committee member Wang Qishan. This pulled in one of 10 deputy directors of the main national planning commission, a former Vice-President of a major state bank and a deputy provincial Party Secretary as well as lesser fry. Officials were told to behave more frugally as we saw in Chapter 2. Anti-corruption measures were extended to the army, where soldiers were instructed to re-use left-over food and to stop selling military numberplates that ensure police do not stop cars carrying them. Delegates to the annual plenary session of the two houses of China's legislature in March 2013 left their high-end fashion accoutrements at home and, in the words of one, went for 'family-style meals. No shark's fin or fancy dishes.'[14]

The campaign had an undoubted effect,

contributing to slower than expected growth in early 2013 as officials held back from launching projects which could expose them. But it aroused a degree of cynicism given the extent of corruption in the system. As with the case against Bo Xilai for 'massive corruption', the high-level targeting involved a measure of politics. Both Bo and Railways Minister Liu were brought down primarily because they had sinned by operating with virtual autonomy from the government. Other culprits lost their political protectors in the leadership transition of 2012–13. No action was taken as a result of the investigations by Bloomberg and the *New York Times* that showed Xi's relatives had amassed assets of $376 million while those of outgoing Premier Wen Jiabao had wealth of $2.7 billion.[15]

The trust deficit is pervasive in a society where deception is rife. Only believe something when the authorities deny it, as the saying goes. Good Samaritans have found themselves successfully sued by those they went to help on the grounds that they must have had an ulterior motive; the Health Ministry was moved to issue a booklet advising the public not to rush to help accident victims. Even the Red Cross Society of China has been hit after discrepancies in figures for sums collected and disbursed for victims of an earthquake in Sichuan

in 2013, setting off a storm of Internet anger. This
came after an episode in which a woman who
claimed to work for the Red Cross flaunted her
wealth, including a Maserati and Hermès hand-
bags, in on-line postings – it turned out to be a hoax
but it was revealing that a lot of people had believed
a charity worker could use public contributions in
such a way. The only true fact on the television
news put out by the state CCTV station is the date,
jokes author Yan Lianke.[16]

The main Shanghai football club was stripped of
its league title and fined for match fixing. A zoo in
Henan which sent its African lion away for breeding
simply substituted a Tibetan mastiff, which, however, gave the game away by barking.[17] Cheating
has become so endemic that in one city where the
authorities imposed controls on final examina-
tions, girls were checked to see whether they had
concealed transmitters in their brassières to enable
them to receive answers to the questions, a measure
that caused their parents to mob the schools in protest. People remember how the authorities tried to
cover up the outbreak of Severe Acute Respiratory
Syndrome (SARS) early this century, the fumbling
reaction to the subsequent outbreak of Avian Flu
and how officials connived at contaminated-blood
collection in Henan which may have infected as

many as 100,000 when Li Keqiang was the provincial Governor. Counterfeiting has become a hallmark of China. Eighty per cent of fake goods seized by US and European Union customs originate in the PRC. As well as foreign luxury items, rip-offs occur in domestic products, including medicines, while phoney colleges with names like foreign universities sell bogus diplomas, some held by officials.

Even sources of China's pride and joy have their hollow aspects. At the opening of the Beijing Olympics, the girl singer was dubbed since the real performer was regarded as insufficiently good-looking and all the 56 children who paraded as representatives of ethnic minorities were Han dressed in colourful disguise. Official data are subject to frequent questioning, with some analysts concluding that they significantly over-state the size of the economy[18] – one recalls Li Keqiang's remark to the US Ambassador in 2007 that the booming statistics were 'man made' and 'only for reference'.[19]

The lack of confidence contributes to a propensity to take direct action in the absence of legal recourse or responsive, accountable local authorities. Social media have facilitated attacks on wayward and corrupt officials, leading in some cases to sanctions. There are estimated to be between 150,000 and 180,000 popular protests each year. Many are peaceful, but some escalate into considerable violence, with crowds of 10,000 or more attacking official buildings and setting police cars on fire. There are also recurrent dramatic acts by individuals who have reached the far borders of frustration, such as the businessman in eastern China who set off three explosions at government offices in his home town after his house was demolished in a road project or the unemployed man fed up with his lot in life who detonated an explosion on a bus in the city of Xiamen which killed 47 people. A man who lost the use of his legs after reportedly being beaten by security agents set off an explosive device at Beijing Airport in the summer of 2013, suffering serious injuries; he explained in a blog posting that he was 'almost without hope, petition road endless'.[20]

For millions of Chinese, the recourse has been to turn to Christianity, Buddhism, Daoism and traditional beliefs such as *feng shui*. The cradle-to-grave 'iron rice bowl' that existed before economic reforms may have been a draconian form of social organization and delivered poor living standards, but it provided a comfort zone for many. Today, the replacement lies outside the system, sometimes to the regime's extreme displeasure, as with the Falun Gong, which has been relentlessly harassed, or in the continuing conflict with the Vatican over the nomination of bishops. One survey showed that half the county-level officials say they believe in divination, face-reading, astrology or interpretation of dreams.[21]

No wonder that the Politburo focuses on what it calls 'social management', acknowledging that 'this is a time when social contradictions are becoming conspicuous in our country'. But the response, so far at least, is inadequate and takes some very knee-jerk forms. The budget for internal security has been increased steeply but official reply to protests has often been to take the course of least resistance, especially when they are mounted by the middle class, which the leadership wants to keep on-side; thus, the authorities in Shanghai, Xiamen on the east coast, Guangdong in the south, Dalian in the northeast and Yunnan in the southwest all cancelled controversial projects or promised reconsideration when people took to the streets. But the regime still reacts with strong-arm tactics when it scents any whiff of a political challenge – an on-line call in 2011 for a Jasmine Revolution in China similar to those in Arab nations brought out only a tiny handful of people but sparked a huge police presence and the hasty removal of an official web posting of Hu Jintao singing a folk song about the flower.

The conciliatory attitude shown when politics is not deemed to be involved is, in its way, a victory for protest. But it leaves key issues unaddressed. The first is where politics stops in China. Consultative Leninism, as this system is sometimes described, is an oxymoron since the Party reserves to itself the right to all decision-making; consultation, in the form of talking to protestors, comes only after the fact. The arbitrary nature of the system remains unaltered. Measures are decided in a closed process without significant public involvement. The enclosed nature of the regime radiates all the way down from the top – the 2012 Party Congress was a prime example of back-room politics with jockeying for position and old power brokers led by Jiang Zemin wheeling themselves out to assert their influence.

The result is the perpetuation of power for the Party State all the way from the leadership compound to Party officials at the grassroots. As society evolves, it becomes increasingly difficult for the authorities and the regime they represent to engage with the people at large. Though they seek information on popular sentiment through frequent opinion surveys, the combination of the size and complexity of the PRC with the omnipotent claims of its ruling apparatus and the lack of space for adaptation of the basic structure produces a growing disconnect between the Party State and its citizens. The system will not implode or explode politically any more than it will collapse economically. But respect for the way the country is run weakens with each food scandal, each day when inhabitants of the capital fear for their lungs, each corruption case, each dent in Xi's China Dream.

5

Why China Will Not Dominate the 21st Century

Set to become the biggest economy on earth in a few years' time, with nuclear weapons, a permanent seat on the UN Security Council, a fast-rising military budget and the world's largest standing army – not to mention an ancient civilization, the biggest population on the planet and a determination to expunge the 'century of humiliation' – there can be no doubt about the way in which China has altered the global balance. But that does not mean it is destined to dominate the world. Indeed, the concept of any one nation ruling the world is even more highly questionable today than it was in the past – and long-range forecasting of any country owning the century must be a highly audacious undertaking.

The previous three chapters explored the domestic limitations which constrain the PRC. These problems are perfectly normal for a country that

101

has come so far, so fast, but they provide a powerful argument against being swept away by Sinomania based on a combination of ancient civilizational claims and crude GDP numbers. China's future involves an array of more subtle factors.

To start with, impressive as it has been, its rise has to be kept in perspective. After the woes it suffered between the mid-19th century and the death of Mao in 1976, China has been coming from a long way back, and the more it progresses, the less the incremental effect of each advance and the greater the complications that envelop it. Chinese commentators say their country deserves equality with the United States. The claim is aided by the climate of declinism in the developed world. The campaign commercial in the 2012 US presidential election depicting a Chinese university lecturer laying out America's decline and concluding 'Now they work for us' fits neatly with the zeitgeist at a time when Gallup reports that Americans are more pessimistic than ever since it started polling on the matter in 1959, and when Europe is sunk in existential despond. But what is fast becoming conventional wisdom begs too many questions – and pessimism tends to be cyclical.

Extrapolation from the last three decades is misleading because it does not take into account the relative simplicity of the first stage of economic growth and the increasing complexity of the second lap. It also assumes that Beijing wants domination. But as Lee Kuan Yew of Singapore has noted, 'The Chinese are in no hurry to displace the US as the Number 1 power in the world and to carry the burden that is part and parcel of that position.'[1]

On the one hand is a country with the world's largest economy, the top destination for international investment in 2013, allies stretching from Japan to the frontiers of Russia – many of them rich and some still growing. Accounting for 39 per cent of global military spending, it enjoys enormous preponderance in weapons systems, a huge capacity for innovation, most of the world's top universities, a reasonably young population, and may even be on the brink of an energy revolution with major economic effects. It has a functioning, if imperfect, legal system, free media and global cultural appeal. Its political system can be dysfunctional, as in logjam over government spending and the budget in 2013, but it provides alternatives and safety valves, and much of its capacity for self-regeneration exists outside the Washington Beltway.

On the other is a state with an economy half the size of the other nation's in nominal terms, ranking 94th globally in purchasing power parity per capita.

Why China Will Not Dominate the Century

It has substantial problems of capital misallocation and excess capacity, weak safety standards, a pollution crisis, endemic corruption, a dependence on imported resources and foreign advanced technology plus a weak record in innovation. Its financial system is fragile and hemmed in with controls. It may possess foreign exchange reserves of more than 3 trillion dollars, but it cannot use the money for domestic purposes because of its financial controls and for fear of setting off a slump from the value of its dollar assets that would undermine this treasure trove.

Despite China's fast-rising military spending, it amounts to only a quarter of that of the United States. The PRC has 22,000 kilometres of borders with 14 states, some of them potentially or actually unstable. The ruling party jealously guards its political control, using repressive means when necessary and wielding the law as a legalist instrument to buttress its rule. Its population is ageing and it faces a mounting range of other social problems. Its army and security apparatus impose Chinese rule on the two huge and recurrently restive territories of Tibet and Xinjiang. Among the permanent members of the Security Council, it is the biggest contributor of non-combat personnel to UN peace-keeping forces and, in 2013, agreed to send fighting troops to help maintain order in Mali, but it plays little role in seeking resolution in major global trouble spots. While the PRC has cooperative associations with many countries which value its assistance, its only formal ally is North Korea. Its constant associations tend to be with poor, troubled nations such as Pakistan and Sudan.

The international record of the United States, from Vietnam through Iraq to Afghanistan, is pitted with failure. But, while China's purchases of raw materials and willingness to accord aid in return without other strings wins plenty of friends, Beijing has not established itself as a geo-political stakeholder commensurate with its economic clout. The PRC unwaveringly insists on its 'core interests', especially in Tibet and Xinjiang, and in the recovery of Taiwan. Retribution is swift for those who transgress: Britain was put into the dog house for more than a year after the Prime Minister, David Cameron, met the Dalai Lama in London in 2012, with ministerial-level visits blocked by Beijing. China brooks no criticism of its human rights record and, again, is ready to take concrete action to show its displeasure – its purchases of Norwegian salmon fell to one-third of the previous level after the dissident Liu Xiaobo was awarded the Nobel Peace Prize in Oslo in 2010. It stresses the importance of non-interference by nations in the affairs of others, but its foreign policy is largely a matter of resources diplomacy conducted on a bilateral, case-by-case basis.

As the major rising state in a world system constituted by the West after the Second World War and reinforced by the fall of the Soviet Union, the PRC is, by nature, a revisionist power. But this involves a paradox for its rise has been made possible by the status quo as regards both its trade and its ability to exclude unwanted external influences. It is understandably miffed by the strong US military presence and the 'island chain' of Washington's allies running from Okinawa through Taiwan to the Philippines. Yet the regional security that has underpinned its export growth depends in the end on the presence of the country from the other side of the Pacific. Beijing resents the way in which the operations of international organizations were set before it emerged from the isolation of the Mao era, but it advances few concrete propositions for change. As the British China watcher Guy de Jonquières put it pithily: 'Over the past three decades, China has shown that it can shake the established world order. It has yet to show that it can help shape a future one.'[2] That may be in keeping with the Sino-centric attitude of the dynastic past, but it hardly points to global dominance for the heirs of the Middle Kingdom.

In Asia, Beijing pursues asymmetrical relationships as it seeks to assert itself as top dog, echoing the tributary states system of the imperial era. But, important as their economic ties are with the mainland area, its neighbours are none too keen to fall in with China's wishes, and have the protective umbrella of the United States to encourage resistance. The effect of the PRC's assertive claims to sovereignty over virtually all the 3.5 million square kilometres of the South China Sea, based on a map dating from 1947, and to a group of uninhabited islands off Japan, on even less convincing grounds, has been to drive the other states involved ever deeper into the arms of Washington. The Obama administration was encouraged to 'pivot' to the Pacific, while the maritime dispute led the Philippines to seek a judgment from a UN tribunal, which Beijing boycotted.[3]

Relations with India, where four-fifths of those polled regard the PRC as a security threat,[4] are scratchy, with a running territorial dispute on the Himalayan frontier and Indian unhappiness about its $40 billion annual trade deficit with the PRC; synergies between Chinese hardware and Indian software spoken of in the 1990s have not materialized. Xi

Jinping has described Russia and China as the 'most important strategic partners' who spoke a 'common language',[5] and they conducted large joint maritime exercises in the summer of 2013. But relations are watchful – the two countries have been engaged in long-running negotiations over gas and Moscow is the mainland's principal arms supplier, but the first has been repeatedly delayed by wrangles over price while Russia has not sold a major weapons system to Beijing for a decade and worries about Chinese economic expansion over the Siberian border.

A survey in 2013 reported that only 5 per cent of Japanese had a positive view of the PRC. After taking office at the end of 2012, the government of Shinzo Abe adopted a far more assertive stance than its predecessors in dealing with the mainland, and, with majorities in both houses of parliament, may try to re-write the constitution to lessen restrictions on military activity while strengthening relations with South-East Asia as a hedge against the PRC. As Chinese and Japanese ships and planes carried out operations around the disputed Senkaku/Diaoyu islands in 2013, there was no shortage of provocations. Japan's biggest naval vessel, a helicopter-carrying destroyer launched in August 2013, carried the same name as a cruiser that had been moored in the International Settlement in

Shanghai during the Sino-Japanese war. A couple of months earlier Abe had been photographed in the pilot's seat of a training jet with the number given to the Japanese biological warfare unit in Manchuria where human guinea pig experiments were conducted on Chinese. Meanwhile Beijing used its sorties into the disputed area to establish a de facto basis for negotiations over a dispute that Deng Xiaoping had shelved in the interests of fruitful relations with Tokyo.

The key global relationship, between China and the United States, is cool or chilly. Each side knows that it needs the other and has every interest in avoiding the 'Thucydides Trap' whereby a rising power and the ruling state come into conflict, like Athens and Sparta in Greece or Germany and Britain in the early 20th century, though parallels between East Asia and pre-1914 Europe are overdone, if only because of nuclear deterrence.[6] But neither trusts the other. The Obama administration has been emboldened to push negotiations for a Trans Pacific Partnership (TPP) free trade zone involving a dozen nations but excluding China; if Japan and South Korea join, it would account for 30 per cent of the global trade in goods and services and would help to set the global rule-book on commerce. Though cross-Strait relations have improved since the Kuomintang recovered Taiwan's presidency in 2008 and Beijing and Taipei agreed to work together, the United States would find it hard not to react if the PLA ever delivered on its latent threat of military action to recover the democratic 'renegade province'.

The G2 concept of 'Chimerica' reflects a reality of the world's two major economies which are interlocked, but it has meant little in terms of forging new co-operative policies. Americans are concerned at the rise of the PRC, the loss of jobs through outsourcing of production to the mainland,[7] Beijing's mercantilist approach to trade and allegations of sharp practice, from currency manipulation through counterfeiting and lack of respect for intellectual property rights to cyber-spying – though revelations in 2013 about their own government's activities may blunt that charge, and China insists that it has 'mountains of data' on cyber-attacks by the United States.

For Beijing, Washington is trying to force it to abide by global rules formulated in the pre-China age while the 'Anyone but China'[8] TPP and the Obama administration's 'Pacific pivot' have all the hallmarks of Cold War containment. Meeting the US President for a short-sleeve summit at a resort in California in mid-2013, Xi linked his 'China Dream' to the 'American Dream', but, in practical terms, the two remain far apart in basic values – even if human rights are little mentioned in public by US administrations these days. A survey in 2013 showed that the proportion of Americans expressing a positive view of the PRC had slumped from 51 to 37 per cent in two years while Chinese good opinions of the United States fell from 58 to 40 per cent.[9]

Xi says the Pacific Ocean is big enough to accommodate the development of two great powers – a perfectly accurate observation, but one which is vitiated by the presence of the US military off China's coast. If the Seventh Fleet was in Guam, there might be more than enough space, but it happens to be in Okinawa, with 60–70 ships, 300 aircraft and 40,000 troops. While Obama said the United States sought 'a new model of cooperation', there was no sign of a shared understanding on what the relationship should be. As for other states in the region, Lee Kuan Yew expresses a widespread view when he says: 'The size of China makes it impossible for the rest of Asia, including Japan and India, to match it in weight and capacity in about 20 to 30 years. So we need America to strike a balance.'[10]

Seen in those terms, the dominance of the PRC appears even more unlikely. China might become economically stronger than the United States –

though this entails a continued weakening of the latter, which is by no means inevitable – but the equation looks different when one lines up America plus a more confident Japan plus India, which may well have the world's biggest population by 2025[11] and have advanced in its messy, democratic manner. Then, from the other side of the world, one must add in the European Union with the largest GDP in the world (more than twice that of China) and its 26 nation-states, including one major power in Germany and two substantial middle rankers in France and Britain. If free trade talks between the United States and the EU reach fruition, and there is a breakthrough in US-backed negotiations for a similar agreement in the Pacific, China risks finding itself with an awkward choice between being an outsider or conforming to rules set, once again, by others which do not favour its economic model.

Then there are other nations round the globe which are not keen on seeing China becoming a hegemon. These countries still have to work out how they are going to deal with the rise of the PRC, and one prospect is for them to cooperate more closely on the basis of shared values. This is not an anti-Chinese coalition but may be facilitated by Beijing's lack of allies. In any case, the scale and momentum of the mainland's growth should not blind us to the strengths of the rest of the world to place in the balance when considering if the rising great power will own the 21st century.

When it comes to 'soft power', where one might expect China's civilizational strengths to make themselves felt, the case for PRC dominance is equally unproven. Yes, there are 700 Confucius Institutes and classrooms round the world teaching Mandarin while the CCTV state network has opened international operations and *China Daily* publishes editions in Europe, North America, Asia and Africa. But few people choose to adopt the Chinese way of life. Confucianism is presented by some of its advocates as a system that puts brute Western ways to shame and has deeply influenced East Asia. But it has little global traction; those seeking to change autocratic systems and to advance their societies to a less inequitable future are more likely to agitate for competitive democracy than for a set of hierarchical behavioural norms which, in the words of a 19th-century follower of the sage, stress 'proper relationships, between ruler and minister, father and son, superiors and subordinates, the high and the low, all in their proper place, just as hats and shoes are not interchangeable'.[12]

Individuals, companies and civil society that thrive in less authoritarian states generally enjoy

113

greater outreach than China's government-directed efforts. A regime which cannot admit to uncomfortable facts in its own history and refuses debate on its assumed truths is hardly in a position to win intellectual support except from those whose appetite for the downfall of the United States was left unrequited by the failure of the Soviet Union. The reason Chinese give for buying foreign-made goods says much about the advantages products of other countries possess – their genuineness, high quality and safety, as well as their brand appeal.[13] There is scant evidence for the thesis that the world will become more Chinese[14] – walk the streets of a mainland city and you will see far more foreign influences, from clothes and magazine covers to fast food outlets and hair styles, than you will find traces of China in the West. English remains the global lingua franca – more people are learning it in the PRC than foreigners are learning Chinese.

Despite their country's increased prosperity, plenty of Chinese seek to move abroad. Apart from North America, Australia and New Zealand, around one million Chinese are estimated to have gone to live in Europe this century, whether legally or illegally. Some 80,000 gained US green cards in 2011. Those who have done well from the system are among the keenest to move. A survey in 2011 found that 27 per cent of Chinese with a net worth of 100 million yuan or more have emigrated or obtained foreign passports or residence permits while another 47 per cent were considering leaving the PRC. An agency in Beijing charges $15,000 or more to advise the well-off on means of gaining foreign residence status. Capital flight in 2011 has been estimated at $600 billion. More than 85 per cent of millionaires polled in 2012 planned to send their children abroad for education – Xi Jinping's daughter went to Harvard (under an assumed name) and Bo Xilai's son attended Harrow school in England, Balliol College at Oxford and the Kennedy School at Harvard.

Warmth for China seems to be somewhat on the wane. The 2013 edition of an annual poll conducted for the BBC put China ninth of 21 nations in terms of positive appreciation, with 42 per cent approval and 39 per cent disapproval – the latter verdict was up eight points since the previous year. Crowds demonstrate for democracy in the Middle East and Africa, but nobody turns out to call for the installation of a Chinese-style system of government. In the PRC itself, the Pew survey of 2012 reported that 52 per cent of those questioned said they liked American ideas on democracy, with only 29 per cent disagreeing – 70 per cent of those in the higher-income category had a positive view. The following year, the Institute found positive views of the United States among 63 per cent of global respondents compared to 50 for China, with 59 per cent regarding the first as a partner compared to 39 per cent for the second.[15]

Even in countries that sell a lot to China and have welcomed its investment in manufacturing as well as natural resources, reservations are surfacing. There are complaints about working practices at Chinese-operated enterprises,[16] with violent clashes erupting in Zambia's copper belt, where the government took over the running of one such mine in 2013 because of safety lapses.[17] Chinese gold miners have been rounded up in Ghana.[18] Lamido Sanusi, the governor of Nigeria's central bank, equates the way in which the PRC takes raw materials from developing nations and sells manufactured goods back to 'opening up a new form of imperialism',[19] while President Jacob Zuma of South Africa has spoken of trade patterns that are 'unsustainable in the long term'.[20] Brazil has brought in regulations to limit Chinese involvement in domestic manufacturing. Some Australian politicians worry about PRC companies buying into their country's mining sector, and of the dangers of the currency becoming dependent on demand from the mainland.

Why China Will Not Dominate the Century

For all its growth, China remains, by its nature, a dependent power, constrained by its reliance on imports of minerals (taking 80 per cent of global supply in 2012), oil (it is set to overtake the United States as the biggest buyer in 2014), gas (as it seeks to reduce reliance on coal for energy) and, in the event of a bad harvest, food or animal feed. This is in striking contrast to the United States in its era of expansion. China has around 20 per cent of the world's population but less than half that in arable land and renewable water and, as we have seen, both these vital resources are under threat.

Despite the flow of headlines about China buying up the world, its major acquisitions outside the raw materials and food industries have been limited. Foreign investment into China remains well ahead of Chinese outward investment, hitting its highest monthly level for more than two years in the summer of 2013. The PRC remains the last great business frontier, especially if the government pushes through the switch to increased consumption. But the slowing of the economy has had a ripple effect – 12 of 18 major US companies with large exposure to the mainland underperformed on the S&P stock market index in the summer of 2013, and those on *The Economist*'s Sinodependency Index, which measures US enterprises by their revenues in China, have dropped steadily since 2009.[21] Many foreign firms have found it harder than expected to penetrate the mainland market and some ran into legal problems as they became targets for anti-trust action as well as grappling with a non-level playing field.[22]

But the economy remains quite dependent on foreign-invested firms, which account for the bulk of Chinese exports of high-technology products. The PRC may have some of the world's biggest companies, which is hardly surprising given its size and growth, but the major world enterprises operating on a global scale are based in the West or Japan. China's big firms do not enjoy international consumer reach, except as anonymous assemblers for foreign brands, and lack the brand image that helps to spread American, European, Japanese and South Korean influence among consumers round the planet.

Such issues have their importance. But the central argument of this book lies, rather, in the nature of the Chinese system of governance, which, given the intense centralization of authority in the Party State, affects everything. The enormous material achievements of the last 35 years have not been matched by a corresponding development of the country's ruling ethos. It would be obtuse to deny the shortcomings of democratic states, but they have also shown a considerable ability to rectify themselves. The danger for the PRC is that the Communist Party straitjacket will inhibit the change the nation needs to continue its ascent. Reaching back into more than two thousand years of often mythical history is no great comfort in this respect, given the degeneration of dynasties – if the Party is the latest occupant of the Dragon Throne, it is all too easy to see it being encircled by the kind of tribulations that brought down the Qin, the Han, the Tang, the Song, the Ming and the Qing. Rather than being a source of strength, the past is replete with pitfalls that the latest holder of the Mandate of Heaven in its Marxist-Leninist-Maoist-market incarnation would do well to avoid.

Indeed, even if the political attitude of its rulers are often redolent of the Middle Kingdom mentality, the country's socio-economic development sets today's China apart from the past in many directions. It is engaged with the world in a way that it has never been before. It has a middle class with aspirations that are closer to those of upwardly mobile human beings anywhere than to behaviour patterns stretching back to the First Emperor and beyond. Technology means that Chinese can communicate with one another in an unprecedented manner. The Party State may seek to retain control of what its citizens say, but the size of the population makes this difficult to enforce and the mere fact of individual exchanges is a major liberalizing step in the emancipation of thought. The traditional belief that allegiance and obeisance of the governed to the governors take precedence over personal interests and ethics holds less and less purchase on citizens.

Such developments are healthy for the evolution of the nation but confront the regime with major challenges, as this book has shown. Xi Jinping's recourse to rule by slogans, complete with his 'mass line' and 'rectification' campaigns, study sessions and self-criticism, demonstrates how difficult it is for a hermetically sealed elite to adapt to the very process set in train with Deng's economic reforms at the end of the 1970s. By the time Xi and Li Keqiang took over in 2012–13, the most important issue for the PRC stemmed from the tension between the need for change and the strength of the status quo built on the material success of the previous 35 years.

Enthusiasts for the China model insist that the system is in a constant process of ameliorative change; the commentator and private equity financier, Eric Li, suggests that the Communist Party is 'the world's leading expert in political reform'.[23] Such a claim is difficult to credit except in terms of a ruling organization which is constantly scrabbling to assert its authority and legitimacy. Its leadership faces a classic paradox, as we have seen throughout this book: it needs to reform in order to rule more effectively, but reform brings with it the threat of weakening the system. After a decade in which the status quo was strengthened, the far-reaching repercussions of necessary change risk shaking the system, in part and as a whole, and resulting in a slowing of the economy – and, most probably, higher inflation.

Strengthening land ownership rights to encourage modernization of agriculture and liberalizing the *hukou* residence registration system would each entail a relaxation of central control. There would have to be significant devolution of revenue-raising powers to local authorities since they would lose the ability to requisition and auction off land and, in cities, would have to provide for millions of new residents moving in from the countryside.

Liberalizing the financial system and interest rates would put pressure on SOEs which have benefited from a cushion of cheap money and subsidies. Opening up the capital account would lead to a flood of money out of China as people sought to diversify their holdings. Freeing the currency would expose the PRC to the ebbs and flows of the global market. Again, the control of the centre would diminish.

Raising energy and water prices to the level at which waste would be eliminated would have a substantial impact on inflation. Introducing an independent legal system would expose vested interests of all kinds to prosecution and would bring an ultimate loss of control as the Communist Party would have to put itself under the law. Granting greater participation by citizens in decision-making, if not competitive democracy, would be a major shock to the system as it would open debate about the history and role of the monopoly political movement which asserts that it knows what is best for the people.

The challenge of such change would be all the greater because of the nature of the PRC, in which everything leads back to the Party State. Remove one or two bricks and the whole edifice could be at threat, or so the power-holders fear. The spectre of Gorbachev and the Bourbon monarchy is never far away. But if action is not taken, the regime risks growing steadily more out of touch with the population, starting with the vital middle class.

So China finds itself at a watershed in which it

needs to change but knows that change will face it with its biggest test since Deng Xiaoping found the way out of the disaster of the Mao era in the late 1970s. This, as we have seen, is not simply a matter of re-modelling the economy but has much wider social implications. As Zhou Qiren, Dean of the National School of Development at Peking University, puts it:

> Without true reform, even bigger trouble will be waiting. First, reforms must be made in certain key areas, such as the orientation of a socialist market economy and progress in the functioning of a social democratic political system. Without tangible signs of advancement on these fronts, conflicts are bound to erupt ... woven into the social fabric of a rising China is a certain disturbing institutional disease. The younger generation is becoming the driving factor in society. Their evaluation of the system, policy and the surrounding environment is different than previous generations – and they also have higher expectations. Finally, because institutional variables are changing too slowly or are absent, a parallel 'extra-judicial' system is taking root. In many ways, the law says one thing while people actually practise something else. Many choose not to abide by the law because it is so unreasonable, while economic regulations are so impracticable that people end up going underground to survive.

The authorities seem to have forgotten that if nothing is to be challenged or reviewed, this will naturally lead to heterodoxy. China is standing before a critical crossroads, where reforms are as difficult as they are necessary. The more that progress is delayed, the harder it becomes.[24]

The success of the China model adopted by Deng bred systemic inertia in the first decade of the present century, just as the endurance of the empire had done for previous dynasties. One can understand why. If progress had been so impressive, why alter the machine? But the result was that everything in the existing apparatus became exaggerated, now as then. Economically, growth got out of hand, and, when it was threatened at the end of 2008, the reaction was to pile on more crude expansionary measures, resulting in a credit boom, huge capital misallocation and further distortions. Politically, despite all Wen Jiabao's talk of liberalization, the Party's grip tightened. Territorially, protests in Xinjiang and on the Tibetan Plateau were put down, but ethnic violence and self-immolations increased. Socially, the disjunctions described in the previous chapter deepened. Internationally, China lunged into confrontations with other regional states and held back from assuming a global role in keeping with its economic strength.

Its resentment at being part of a global system whose rules it did not frame is generally underestimated in the West, which set those rules and is happy with them. The belief in Washington and elsewhere that all that is required is for the PRC to operate by those standards, as if they had the everlasting sanctity of tablets of global law, is extremely short-sighted. But, equally, Beijing's failure to put forward discussable alternatives risks relegating it to the status of a querulous outsider in a world system it has joined and needs, but with which it has not really engaged beyond short-term advantage. Given China's economic weight and the lasting change it has brought to the international balance, this is potentially very dangerous; the big outsider is never a good factor for others, or, in the end, for itself, and its size and exclusion, real or perceived, can lead to escalating conflict that imperils all.

The result is a watershed which will determine the course the country takes in this decade and beyond. The accumulation of problems listed in this book are, in a sense, hardly surprising, given the extent of development and the priorities adopted since 1978 and do not, in themselves, point to the coming collapse of China, given the resources of the Party State.

But they are now piling up in a dangerous fashion

and there may not be much time to deal with the combination of pressures. Decision-making will be difficult for a leadership which has long avoided hard choices and is hemmed in by the cocoon of embedded Party rule. If reform is not undertaken in a far-reaching manner, the PRC will lurch from problem to problem, limiting its future development. If change is grasped, there will be a protracted period of difficult transition which will affect the system built up since 1949. Either way, these domestic factors will constrain the extension of the country's global influence as the leadership focuses on internal matters. Domination of the 21st century is not in prospect when the prime concern will be to keep the 'China Dream' alive at home.

Further Reading

The case for Chinese global dominance is put most strongly by Martin Jacques in *When China Rules the World* (London: Allen Lane, 2009; second edition, 2012), though the author himself says the 'catchy' title should not be taken too literally. A number of earlier books had charted China's rise, starting almost two decades ago with Jim Rohwer's *Asia Rising* (New York: Simon & Schuster, 1995). The argument for a Chinese crash was first advanced, to my knowledge, by Gordon Chang in *The Coming Collapse of China* (New York: Random House, 2001), though the forecast in the title has not, of course, come to pass.

The two sides in the debate on whether the 21st century will belong to China were represented by Niall Ferguson and David Daokui Li (for) and Fareed Zakaria and Henry Kissinger (against) in the Munk Debate in Toronto in 2011 – the audience voted 62 per cent against the motion (*http://www.munkdebates.com/debates/china*). Timothy Beardson gives a comprehensive account of the PRC's weaknesses and strengths in *Stumbling Giant* (New Haven: Yale University Press, 2013), while Minxin Pei's *China's Trapped Transition* (Cambridge, MA: Harvard University Press, 2008) remains highly apposite.

Among the flood of books on China, Richard McGregor's *The Party* (London: Allen Lane, 2010) gives the best description and analysis of the political system. *Red Capitalism* by Carl Walter and Fraser Howie (London: John Wiley, 2010) is a penetrating analysis of the financial system. Jonathan Watts provides an excellent survey of the ecological disaster in *When a Billion Chinese Jump* (London: Faber & Faber, 2010). Leslie Chang's *Factory Girls* (London: Picador, 2010) presents superb reportage on migrant workers. Arne Odd Westad's *Restless Empire* (London: Bodley Head, 2012) covers China's relations with the world since 1750, while David Shambaugh's *China Goes Global* (Oxford: Oxford University Press, 2013) presents the PRC as a 'partial power'. Lee Kuan Yew delivers his judgments on China, the US and the future in interviews with Graham Allison, Robert D. Blackwill and

Ali Wyne in *Lee Kuan Yew: The Grand Master's Insights on China, the United States and the World* (Cambridge, MA: MIT Press, 2013). Peter Nolan provides a salutary corrective to the China outward investment story in *Is China Buying the World?* (Cambridge: Polity, 2012). The global spread of Chinese business is reported comprehensively in *China's Silent Army* by Juan Pablo Cardenal and Heriberto Araujo (London: Allen Lane, 2013).

Ezra Vogel's *Deng Xiaoping and the Transformation of China* (Cambridge, MA: Harvard University Press, 2011) gives a monumental account of the man who changed the world. Frank Dikötter's two books, *Mao's Great Famine* (London: Bloomsbury, 2010) and *The Tragedy of Liberation* (London: Bloomsbury, 2013), lay out in forensic detail the horrific human cost of the Great Helmsman's policies and ambition. Roderick MacFarquhar's three-volume *Origins of the Cultural Revolution* (New York: Columbia University Press, 1974–99) and the following volume with Michael Schoenhals, *Mao's Last Revolution* (Cambridge, MA: Belknap Press, 2008), remain the best account of the politics of that era.

For those in a hurry and seeking expert guidance, Jeffrey Wasserstom's *China in the 21st Century* (Oxford: Oxford University Press, 2010) answers most of the questions people ask about China in 135 pages, while Rana Mitter provides *Modern China; A Very Short Introduction* (Oxford: Oxford University Press, 2008). My own books, *The Penguin History of Modern China* (London: Penguin, 2009, second edition, 2013) and *Tiger Head, Snake Tails: China Today* (London: Simon & Schuster, updated paperback edition, 2013), cover China past and present.

Notes

Chapter 1 China's Watershed

1 Statecraft is a term used by Henry Kissinger, *On China* (London: Penguin, 2012).

2 Ibid., p. 493.

3 *http://uk.reuters.com/article/2010/12/06/us-china-economy-wikileaks-idUSTRE6B527D20101206* (accessed 6 August 2013).

4 Ezra Vogel, *Deng Xiaoping and the Transformation of China* (Cambridge, MA: Harvard University Press, 2011), p. 218.

5 Frank Dikötter gives a comprehensive account of the disasters Mao brought: Frank Dikotter, *The Tragedy of Liberation* (London: Bloomsbury, 2013).

6 *PLA Daily*, 22 May 2013; Xi press conference, Rancho Mirage California, 10 June 2013.

7 The formulation, originated by Goldman Sachs, seems in the wrong order given China's weight, but the earlier formulation of CRIB was regarded as less easily marketable.

8 *Financial Times*, 11 April 2013.

9 *Economist*, 18 June 2013.

10 China Outbound Tourism Research Institute quoted in *Financial Times*, 21 May 2013.

11 *Foreign Policy*, 7 February 2013.

12 Ferguson, *http://www.munkdebates.com/debates/ china* (accessed 7 August 2013). Jacques said subsequently of his book: 'The title shouldn't be taken literally. . . . You need a catchy title that's provocative and makes you think.' But he identified his theme as 'the rise of China to a point where it becomes the dominant global power and what that will be like, how it will exercise its hegemony and how that will differ from the Western era, particularly the American era'. *http://www.martinjacques.com/ category/when-china-rules-the-world/interviews/asia -interviews/taiwan-asia-interviews/* (accessed 7 August 2013).

13 *http://www.pewglobal.org/2013/07/18/global-image -of-the-united-states-and-china/* (accessed 7 August 2013).

14 Minxin Pei, *China's Trapped Transition* (Cambridge, MA: Harvard University Press, 2008).

15 World Bank, *http://www.worldbank.org/en/country/ china/overview*; for 'middle-income debate' see *economist.com/middleincome13* (both accessed 7 August 2013).

16 Professor Nailene Chou Wiest in *Caixin*, 14 September 2012: *http://english.caixin.com/2012-09- 14/100438129.html* (accessed 7 August 2013).

17 Tom Holland, *South China Morning Post*, 14 February 2013.
18 *The Economist*, 10 August 2013.
19 National Science Foundation, quoted in *The Economist*, 6 July 2013.
20 AFP, August 2013.
21 *http://www.migrationinformation.org/feature/display.cfm?ID=838* (accessed 7 August 2013).

Chapter 2 The Political Trap

1 *http://www.best-news.us/news-4984826-Xi-Jinping:-garbage-is-misplaced-resources.html* (accessed 12 August 2013).
2 *http://news.yahoo.com/chinas-xi-harks-back-mao-party-cleanup-125352017.html* (accessed 12 August 2013).
3 For new leadership see *China Leadership Monitor*: *http://www.hoover.org/publications/china-leadership-monitor/about* (accessed 12 August 2013).
4 *Le Monde*, 12 May 2013.
5 *Red Flag*, 21 May 2013: *http://cmp.hku.hk/2013/05/22/33193/* (accessed 12 August 2013).
6 *Xinhua*, 24 May 2013.
7 Richard McGregor, *The Party* (London: Allen Lane, 2010), p. 1.
8 *People's Daily*, 22 May 2013.
9 *Caixin*, 10 December 2012: *http://english.caixin.com/2012-12-10/100470648.html* (accessed 12 August 2013).

10 *New York Times*, 19 July 2013: *http://www.nytimes.
com/2013/07/20/world/asia/survey-in-china-shows-
wide-income-gap.html?_r=0* (accessed 12 August
2013).

Chapter 3 Inflection Point

I am grateful to my colleague Larry Brainard for this
apposite phrase.

1 *http://www.worldbank.org/en/news/press-release/
2012/02/27/china-case-for-change-on-road-t-030*
(accessed 12 August 2013).
2 *Neue Zürcher Zeitung*, 24 May 2013.
3 *http://www.grey-water.com/sitebuildercontent/
sitebuilderfiles/ChinaWaterShortage.pdf* (accessed
20 August 2013).
4 IMF *http://www.imf.org/external/np/sec/pr/2013/pr
13192.htm* (accessed 12 August 2013). *Financial
Times*, 18 July 2013.
5 *Wall Street Journal*, 26 June 2013.
6 *Guardian*, 17 March 2013: *http://www.theguardian.
com/world/2013/mar/17/china-premier-li-keqiang-
bureaucracy* (accessed 20 August 2013).
7 Kevin Lau and Stephen Green, *China Daily*, 6 May
2013.
8 *http://news.xinhuanet.com/english/china/2013-07/20/
c_132558552.htm?utm_source=Sinocism+Newsletter
&utm_campaign=4bf43bd340-Sinocism07_21_13
&utm_medium=email&utm_term=0_171f237867-
4bf43bd340-29592865* (accessed 12 August 2013).
9 Usha Haley and George Haley, *Subsidies to*

Chinese Industry (Oxford: Oxford University Press, 2013).

10 Ruchir Sharma, *Wall Street Journal*, 27 June 2013.

11 China Health and Retirement Longitudinal Survey, 2013.

12 *http://www.imf.org/external/np/sec/pr/013/pr13192.htm* (accessed 12 August 2013).

13 *Financial Times*, 21 May 2013.

14 *The Economist*, 5 January 2013.

15 *http://www.imf.org/external/np/sec/pr/2013/pr131 92.htm* (accessed 12 August 2013).

Chapter 4 Behind the Dream

1 *The Economist*, 6 July 2013.

2 China Research Center on Aging, 2013; Poverty line, China Health and Retirement Longitudinal Study, 2013.

3 *http://www.scmp.com/news/china/article/1250966/survey-shows-problems-mainlands-growing-elderly-population* (accessed 13 August 2013).

4 Yanzhong Huang, *YaleGlobal*, 6 June 2013; Proceedings of the National Academy of Sciences, 2013. *New York Times*, 8 July 2013: *http://www.nytimes.com/2013/07/09/world/asia/pollution-leads-to-drop-in-life-span-in-northern-china-study-finds.html?ref=proceedingsofthenationalacademyof sciences&_r=0* (accessed 20 August 2013).

5 *http://www.ctsu.ox.ac.uk/research/mega-studies/smoking-china-retrospective/three-million-tobacco-*

deaths-a-year-in-china-by-middle-of-next-century
(accessed 20 August 2013).

6 *Nature,* 3 July 2013.
7 *http://damsandalternatives.blogspot.co.uk/2013/05/
   ft-water-shortages-in-china-and-three.html* (accessed
   13 August 2013).
8 For the origins and costs of the environmental crisis,
   see Elizabeth Economy, 'The Great Leap Backwards',
   Foreign Affairs, September/October 2007.
9 *Wall Street Journal,* 23 May 2013.
10 *China Daily,* European edition, 19–25 August 2011.
11 *Wall Street Journal,* 1 August 2013.
12 *http://carnegieendowment.org/2007/11/20/corruption-
   in-china-how-bad-is-it/2028* (accessed 13 August
   2013).
13 *http://chinadigitaltimes.net/2009/09/video-six-years-
   old-i-want-to-be-a-currupted-official-when-i-grow-
   up/* (accessed 16 August 2013).
14 *Wall Street Journal,* 15 March 2013.
15 *Bloomberg,* 29 June 2012: *http://www.bloom
   berg.com/news/2012-06-29/xi-jinping-millionaire-rel
   ations-reveal-fortunes-of-elite.html;New York Times,*
   25 October 2012: *http://www.nytimes.com/2012/
   10/26/business/global/family-of-wen-jiabao-
   holds-a-hidden-fortune-in-china.html?pagewanted=
   all&_r=0* (both accessed 13 August 2013).
16 Yan Lianke, Asia House, London, 21 May 2013.
17 *http://www.bbc.co.uk/news/world-asia-china-23714
   896* (accessed 16 August 2013).
18 See, for example, Christopher Balding, SSRN paper:
   http://ssrn.com/abstract=2307054; Michael Pettis on

the growth debate: *http://blog.mpettis.com/2013/08/the-changing-debate-over-chinas-economy/*; and Patrick Chovanec: *http://www.theguardian.com/world/2012/mar/22/china-economy-hard-landing* (all accessed 16 August 2013).

19 *http://wikileaks.org/cable/2007/03/07BEIJING1760.html* (accessed 13 August 2013).

20 *http://www.bbc.co.uk/news/world-asia-china-23388 448* (accessed 13 August 2013).

21 *New York Times*, 13 May 2013.

Chapter 5 Why China Will Not Dominate the 21st Century

1 *Lee Kuan Yew: The Grand Master's Insights on China, the United States and the World*, interviews and selections by Graham Allison, Robert D. Blackwill and Ali Wyne (Cambridge, MA: MIT Press, 2013), p. 11.

2 See *China's Geoeconomic Strategy*, LSE Ideas, June 2012.

3 *http://www.pewglobal.org/2013/07/18/global-image-of-the-united-states-and-china/* (accessed 13 August 2013).

4 *The Economist*, 25 May 2013.

5 *http://www.bbc.co.uk/news/world-asia-china-21873 944* (accessed 13 August 2013).

6 Graham Allison, *Financial Times*, 22 August 2012.

7 As epitomized by Peter Navarro's 2012 television documentary *Death by China*.

8 David Pilling, *Financial Times*, 22 May 2013.
9 As note 3.
10 *Lee Kuan Yew*, p. 40.
11 New York Times, 15 December 2009: *http://www. nytimes.com/2009/12/16/world/asia/16census.html* (accessed 16 August 2013).
12 Zeng Guofan, 'Proclamation against the Bandits', 1854: *https://www2.stetson.edu/secure/history/hy30 8C01/zengguofan.html* (accessed 16 August 2013).
13 *Financial Times*, 3 June 2013.
14 *http://www.martinjacques.com/books/* (accessed 13 August 2013).
15 As note 3.
16 Chinese work practices are documented by Juan Pablo Cardenal and Heriberto Araujo in *China's Silent Army* (London: Allen Lane, 2013).
17 *http://www.bbc.co.uk/news/business-21520478* (accessed 13 August 2013).
18 *Guardian*, 24 April 2013.
19 *Financial Times*, 11 March 2013: *http://www.ft.com/ mhtml#axzz2YGHzD0bR* (accessed 13 August 2013).
20 China–Africa Forum, Beijing, 19 July 2013.
21 *The Economist*, 20 July 2013.
22 *http://www.reuters.com/assets/print?aid=USBRE96I 06620130719* (accessed 13 August 2013).
23 *http://www.ted.com/talks/eric_x_li_a_tale_of_two_ political_systems.html*. The ensuing debate on democracy, in which Li's arguments are taken to task by Yasheng Huang of the MIT Sloan School of Management, is at *http://blog.ted.com/2013/07/01/*

why-democracy-still-wins-a-critique-of-eric-x-lis-a-tale-of-two-political-systems/ (both accessed 13 August 2013).

24 *Caixin*, 1 July 2013: *http://english.caixin.com/2013-07-01/100550000.html* (accessed 20 August 2013).